TAKE THE WHEEL

Take the Wheel

A Woman's Guide to Buying a Car Her Own Damn Self

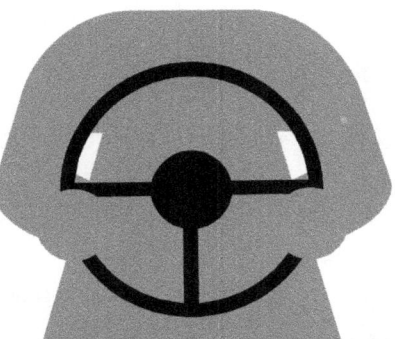

Second Edition

KRISTEN HALL-GEISLER

Practical Fox
Portland, Oregon

Take the Wheel: A Woman's Guide to Buying a Car Her Own Damn Self–
Second Edition

Practical Fox, Portland, Oregon

© 2017
All rights reserved. First edition published 2013. Second edition 2017.

Cover image by Spot Color Marketing

Editing and production by Indigo Editing & Publications.

Paperback ISBN: 978-0-9893658-6-4
eBook ISBN: 978-0-9893658-7-1

Library of Congress Control Number: 2013908554

This one's for my Nerd Girls.

CONTENTS

Preface ix
Introduction 1

Part One: Arm Yourself 10
Creating Your Budget 11
Budgeting for Insurance, Sort Of 19
Gas and Maintenance 23
Wait! Do You Even Need a Car? 25

Part Two: Let's Go Shopping! 29
Climbing the Decision Tree 31
Questions to Ask Yourself 35
Types of Vehicles 39
Technology 45
Other Considerations 49
Back to the Budget 51
If You Decide You Want New 53
If You Decide You Want Used 57
Leasing a Car 63
Online Shopping 65
TrueCar 69
Craigslist 71
Apps 73

At the Dealership 75
Drive It Like You Own It 79

Special Section: Your Guide to Green(er) Cars 87
It's Pretty Easy Being Green 89
What Is a Hybrid? 93
What Is a Plug-In Hybrid? 97
What Is an Electric Vehicle? 101
What Is a Hydrogen Vehicle? 107
What Is a Diesel Vehicle? 111
What Is E85? 115
What Is a Liquid Natural Gas Vehicle? 119
Conclusion 121

Part Three: Bringing Baby Home 123
Starting the Conversation 125
Negotiation Lite 131
Wading through the Paperwork 135
Warranties and Service Contracts 137
It's Yours! Now What? 141
Maintenance 143
If You Make a Mistake 149
Lemon Laws 151
Nobody's Fault but Mine 153
Epilogue 157

The 5 Questions Section 159
Acknowledgments 161
Bibliography 163

Preface

In 2014, I published my first book, *Take the Wheel: A Woman's Guide to Buying a Car Her Own Damn Self*. It sold pretty well for a first book on a niche subject, and I was happy to let it roll along.

In the meantime, I continued with my work as a freelance automotive journalist specializing in automotive technology and the future of transportation. I knew *Take the Wheel* would get outdated, but I also knew that the automotive industry moves very slowly. It takes a minimum of five years to create a car from drawing board to showroom. Think of everything that has to be designed, manufactured, coordinated, tested for safety, and bolted onto or into the car on the assembly line. Every wire, every mirror, every line of code (Volkswagen, we're looking at you) is created by someone and brought together to create a vehicle. It's amazing it only takes a few years.

But technology moves at the speed of light. Startups can announce themselves, raise millions of dollars, burn through the money, and crash into oblivion faster than a traditional automaker can design a home screen for the infotainment center in the console. People want that technology, they want those apps, they want that kind of speed inside their cars. They want Waze and Spotify and voice-to-text and everything else. Automakers have never been in the tech business, and when they try to do it all themselves, it turns out it doesn't work as well as the real-deal apps do. Customers end up setting their phones in the cup holders and finding workarounds for the baked-in systems that came with their cars.

That's not to mention the other technological advances that are happening. Ride sharing, car sharing, advance driving assistance, self-parking—automakers are equipped to tackle basically none of this on their own. They need those startups that manufacture lidar sensors and created artificial intelligence algorithms. So they've been creating partnerships and investing money to bring that technology into the cars people want far faster than they could do it alone in their car-making towers.

I couldn't talk about changes in the auto industry without talking about Tesla. When I was writing the first edition of *Take the Wheel*, the company had stopped production of the Tesla Roadster two-seater and was behind on deliveries of its new Model S sedan. This was before the Model S earned a perfect score from *Consumer Reports*, before autonomous driving software was part of an over-the-air update for Tesla owners, before the Ludicrous Mode over-the-air software update made the already fast Model S go even faster, before they were valued more highly than Ford by the stock market. It was also before the autopilot scandal and before the Model X SUV with its poor construction quality. Tesla's electric vehicles have created the halo effect that EVs needed in order to seem doable, even desirable. Automakers had to step up their game in the EV space as

Preface

well. Because Tesla raised the bar so high, no one has yet cleared it.

With all of these changes, it was time for a new edition of *Take the Wheel*. I've cut some flabby parts and improved some financial parts. I also included the text of *Alternative Fueliverse*, my booklet on any kind of powertrain that isn't a gasoline-powered internal combustion engine. You'll find it here in the section called "Your Guide to Green(er) Cars." I've updated the sections on being carless to include things like car-sharing options, and I updated the diesel section to talk about the VW scandal and its effects on your ability to buy a diesel car.

A lot has changed in the last four years, but most American women still rely on cars we own to get around. We still control most of the big-ticket household purchases, and we still make up more than half of the registered drivers in this country. We also do a lot of research at home before setting foot in a dealership, which makes us more informed about the particular car we want to buy than the salesperson probably is. But that doesn't stop them from talking down to us, asking if our husband is okay with us spending so much money, and generally being asshats to us when all we want to do is give them thousands of dollars and drive away as fast as we possibly can from the dealership.

I hope the new, revised, expanded, and improved edition of *Take the Wheel* is even more helpful than the original. Good luck out there!

Introduction

What you know — or don't know – about cars has nothing to do with being female. It has nothing to do with where you fall on the sociosexual-gender spectrum at all, from platform stiletto-wearing man killer to flannel shirt-wearing lady killer. It most certainly has nothing to do with your reproductive organs, which determine your sex. It has everything to do with car lust. Some people have it; lots of people don't.

I am a full-fledged, card-carrying woman. I am wearing a cute dress and Betsey Johnson lingerie as I type in my pink office (paint name: Temptress). I am also a car expert. I grew up in a family that always had annual tickets to NASCAR races and in a home with more cars than licensed drivers. Now, I professionally test-drive and review cars, from emissions-free electric cars that couldn't get out of their own way to gas-guzzling exotic cars that scare other cars into the slow lane with a blip of the throttle.

Even the girliest of girls know what cars they like. They know if they like the eco-friendly(ish) Ford Fusion Hybrid sedan or the adorable – and parkable – BMW i3 compact electric car, which looks like something that might be able to land on Mars. Some like the monster Dodge Challenger

Take The Wheel

SRT with its powerful engine and heavy shifter, and some like the runs-like-a-top, top-down Mazda MX-5 Miata. Pickups, hatchbacks, minivans, sedans—whatever a woman wants to drive, it's out there.

But for, oh, about a hundred years, women have been told that cars aren't really their arena. Cars are big. They're mechanical. They're expensive. Buying one involves math—*ew*. This despite the fact that by the end of 2012, for the first time ever, there were more women registered to drive than men. An American woman will keep her new car for, on average, 6.5 years. She'll even keep a used car for an average of 5.3 years. Her monthly car payment will linger longer than the in-laws during Christmas vacation, with loan terms averaging sixty-seven months. Typically, by the time her car loan is paid off, it could enter first grade.

Modern women make the big-ticket buying decisions in about eight out of ten households, whether they're single, married, partnered, polygamous, or whatever. They've got money and intelligence; what they don't have is practice buying cars, especially not solo. This is one of those areas, like construction work and wearing the same underwear two days in a row, that we still mostly leave to men. We cook, clean, pick up the kid, scoop the litter box, take the dog to the vet, have our own damn jobs, and coordinate schedules for everyone in the house, including adults who know perfectly well how to use Google Calendar but can't seem to enter events in any kind of meaningful, shared way. Can't someone else at least buy the stupid car every few years?

Men can, of course, buy the stupid car. But so can women. It's a hassle no matter where you fall on the gender

Introduction

continuum. If you can do the research and buy a refrigerator (How big? How energy efficient? How expensive? Will it fit in the current slot, or do I have to remodel the kitchen?), you can do the research and buy a car (same questions, more options, no remodeling the kitchen). Research by Autotrader.com showed that in 2010, women influenced 80 percent of all vehicle purchases, and they were the sole buyers of more than half of all vehicles. Think about it: *more than half* of the vehicles bought in 2010 were purchased by women who bought the damn things themselves. According to a Polk survey of US vehicle registrations, 38.5 percent of cars were registered to women as of March 2011. But that Autotrader.com survey also found that 75 percent of women "don't feel certain or sure of themselves when visiting dealerships." So we're buying cars in droves, and yet we still feel uncomfortable with the process.

That's where I come in. I'll help you decide if you even need a car (urbanites can save big with a bike and a transit pass, or even a car-sharing account). I'll help you create a budget for the car you want, shop online and in person for new and used versions of that car, test-drive it with aplomb, navigate the negotiation process without feeling like a brainless idiot, and take care of that new vehicle like your livelihood depends on it. Because in most of the United States, where commutes to and from work take an average of fifty minutes total every day, it kind of does.

What you need is a friend to give you the know-how and the confidence to get through this process without tens of thousands of dollars of buyer's remorse adding to the insomnia you already have. A friend to tell you that not so many men really know that much about cars anymore, either. A friend to tell you that it's time for the school of thought claiming that women get taken advantage of to be retired—really, it should have disappeared with the belt-on maxi pad. That friend is me.

Cars give women a measure of freedom to work, to travel, to conduct business. But I don't mean to say with this book that every woman needs a car of her own. Lots of women share one car with their partner. And lots of women, especially younger women in urban areas, share cars through networks like car2go, ReachNow, or Zipcar, or they use peer-to-peer sharing networks like Getaround and Turo.

So a car of one's own isn't the point. Nor is the point that if guys can lust after cars and give them girls' names and transfer their sexual power (or lack thereof) to cars, then women should be able to do all those stereotypically masculine things, too. Though if you want to buy a 500-hp Shelby Mustang and name it Brenda, I will think you are a total badass and want to be your friend. The point is that a woman needs to make a decision of her own and be comfortable and confident with that decision, whether that means leasing a car for three years, buying a car and driving it until the engine gives up and dies 200,000 miles later, or skipping the whole headache and getting a monthly bus pass.

Remember, women have at least some say in the purchase of 80 percent of the cars parked in America's driveways, and nearly half of the cars on the road are registered in women's names. Clearly most of us have a need for a car

Introduction

of our own, whether we're married, single, or somewhere in between. But many women, even smart, professional, otherwise-totally-on-top-of-their-shit women, are filled with dread at the prospect of jumping through all the hoops required to buy a car. They bring along a husband, boyfriend, dad, or neighbor—anyone that the salesperson will actually look in the eye.

In the course of researching this book, I did lots of formal and informal interviews, and often the men I talked to said the one thing I should make sure I put in the book is that a woman should "take someone with her." By which they meant she should take a man with her.

"I think you misunderstand the premise of the book," I would say. I would explain again that *Take the Wheel* will help women, who are smart and capable and income-earning in their own right, to buy a car without bringing along a penis to make themselves seem legit.

"That's reality," the men would say. To my face. Sometimes they would backpedal, with some version of "Well, not you, of course. You're a car person."

I am a car person, but car buying is just as annoying to me as it is to almost anyone. And I'm not that special; we all manage to budget for our apartments, our smartphone bills, our vintage Coach bags. If we can do that, we can buy a car. I am going to change this boys-only reality the men keep telling me about, and you are going to help me do it.

One thing is definitely in our favor. Dealerships are moving more toward internet and app-based sales rather than face-to-face haggling sessions. This move to digital sales appeals to men and women alike, as it allows for maximum research at home and minimum time in an uncomfortable plastic chair in a dealership with a migraine-inducing fluorescent light blinking overhead. As women move into more management and design positions at car companies, the products are getting more woman-friendly, which has been shown to be more man-friendly, too. It turns out that the things women want in a car are the things human beings want in a car. Crazy!

There are a few differences in how women make purchases versus how men do it, according to Sheryl Connelly, who has been manager of Ford Global Consumer Trends and Futuring for more than a decade. In her research of worldwide trends, she's found that women have a couple of triggers when it comes to buying.

One is "tactical consumption," in which women take into account the values a company projects and how those values will reflect on them. A company that seems to be in line with a woman's own values is more likely to get her business, whether that's based on family values, animal rights, sustainability, or any other value a woman might hold close to her heart. In the noncar world, TOMS Shoes and fair-trade coffee have seen the positive effects of this trigger, Connelly noted. For cars, it may be a hybrid or an electric car that's better for the planet that makes a difference, or it might be a landfill-free manufacturing plant, or even a car company that donates to schools or science competitions.

An adjacent trend Connelly sees is the "careful consumer." After the economic collapse of 2008, conventional wisdom

Introduction

> **FUN FACT**
>
> The BMW Z4 convertible got a complete overhaul in 2009—by a team composed entirely of women designers, and it won the EyesOn Design Award for Best Production Vehicle at the Detroit Auto Show that year. I clapped like crazy when the woman who headed that project stepped onto the stage to accept her statue and say nice things about her team in a German accent. No one that I've heard has cursed this curvy, low-slung, sexy little car with the "chick car" epithet, which to my mind proves that women like hot, fast cars as much as men do.

said that people would cut back on all spending and only buy the cheapest goods. They would no longer pay a premium, the thinking went. Not true, says Connelly. "I think people will hold on to their values, and they'll scrimp and splurge to do that." So women are buying fewer things, but they're saving up to buy the one great thing that fits their needs perfectly and maybe has a little bit of luxury. This explains the automotive trend to outfit small cars that have great fuel economy with luxury touches like leather seats, high-end sound systems, or state-of-the-art safety technology. Women will buy the best they can afford without compromising what they value—as long as they feel confident in how to do that. This book is meant to give you that confidence. Take the wheel!

Part One: Arm Yourself

Before we talk about negotiations, before you take a test drive, even before you hop on the internet to research cars you like, you need to crunch some numbers. If you do it now, the rest of the process is so much easier. Trust me.

Creating Your Budget

I can see it floating over your head in a thought balloon like a cartoon character: you've already got a car in mind. It's a roadster. It's a minivan. It's a muscle car. It's a twenty-five-year-old Toyota Corolla that your uncle said he'd sell you for three hundred bucks, which makes me sad. You can dream bigger than a moldy Corolla, surely.

Pack your daydream thought bubble away for now. We'll cover which car you'll buy in the next part. First, we need to set up a budget. Once you know what you can afford—and no more—you can find a car that satisfies your need for safety, gadgetry, power, and style.

First, assess how much money you've got coming in to your bank account and how much is flowing out each month. This is a pain in the ass, but it must be done. Your income should be pretty easy to figure out, especially if you've got a regular salary. If you're paid hourly and your hours vary, or if you're a freelancer paid by the project, average your total income each month to find a reasonable starting point. Then subtract your debt payments: rent or mortgage, student loans, credit card payments. In an ideal world, the debt payments eat up less than 45 percent of your gross income each month.

Take The Wheel

An example:

Income: $4,000 per month before taxes
Mortgage: $1,000 per month, including taxes and insurance
Student loans: $250 per month
Credit card: $100 per month

This hypothetical (and very responsible, it seems) person spends $1,350, or 33 percent of her income, each month on debt payments, which leaves money for groceries, utilities, savings, clothes, and—hooray!—a car. If she wanted to hit that 45 percent mark for total loan payments, she could spend another $450 a month on a car payment. Pretty reasonable, really.

If your expenses are low because you live off the grid in a national forest or you're still happily ensconced in your parents' basement, you can spend more on a car. If your rent alone eats up 45 percent of your paycheck, you might want to check out a monthly bus pass or buying a sweet bike instead. (Living car-free can be done; see the "Wait! Do You Even Need a Car?" section later in this chapter for more if you're tossing that idea around.)

Unless you've been saving up for a while to buy a car with cash, you're going to need a loan. Most car loans come from either a bank, credit union, or the financial arm of the car company; whatever way you choose, you'll be paying interest on the amount of money you borrow. The interest will be based on market conditions, how long you're going to take to pay back the loan, and what kind of credit risk you are. A thirty-six-month loan will usually

Creating Your Budget

have a lower interest rate than a sixty-month loan, but the monthly payments will be higher. A buyer with a shoddy history of paying her bills and a line of collections agents beating on her apartment door will have a higher interest rate than a buyer who has paid her bills on time every month since she was a college senior. If you're anything like the average American, who keeps her car for six years or so, a sixty-month loan will allow you to pay the car off and then save up for a year. You can either pay off some other debts to help out your credit, or you can use that money as a down payment on the next car to keep your payments reasonable.

Your credit risk or worthiness is what everybody's talking about when they say "credit score." These magical and somewhat mysterious numbers are generated independently by three companies—Experian, Equifax, and TransUnion—and they each have different scoring models. That's right—you can have several different credit scores, though they should all be sort of close. This score isn't the only thing a lender will look at, but it is pretty important. Think of credit scores as having the same bearing on your car loan as your SAT scores had on your college admissions. It's not the thing that gets you accepted, but it's an easy way to cut you from the list if the number is really, really low.

The companies that create these credit scores in their super-secret number-crunching laboratories inside island volcano lairs aren't very forthcoming about how they come up with these numbers. At all. But they have loosened their grip on the number itself, which makes it easier for you to monitor and improve if you can. Many banks and credit card companies offer a free peek at your credit score every month or so, though it probably won't dig into any details. To see your full credit report, visit annualcreditreport.com. That's the only website authorized by the federal government to provide a free credit report as required by the Fair Credit Reporting Act. You are entitled to one free credit report from each of the major credit reporting agencies every year. Other sites may try to sell you something—or they may collect your information and sell it on to someone else.

If your bills are paid and your credit cards aren't out of hand, you'll probably have a score in the same range as the calories in a large chocolate milkshake, maybe 750 or 800. If there are pages and pages of letters from collection agencies, loan applications denied, and credit card balances higher than your annual income, your score will likely be closer to the calories in two pieces of dry toast.

Once you've seen your score or flipped through the full report, which is a tad intimidating in itself, find an auto loan calculator. Autotrader.com and Cars.com both have calculators that work fine for finding typical new and used auto interest rates for your estimated score. The lowest credit scores can translate to interest rates four times higher than the best rates. You'll want to know this long before you sign on any dotted lines.

Let's go back to our hypothetical buyer with the $450 monthly car payment budget and say she's imperfect like most of us but not too badly in over her head. She probably missed some student loan payments a couple of years back. We'll say she's got a credit score of 675. According

Creating Your Budget

to the calculator on the day I checked, that gets her an interest rate of 6.4 percent for a sixty-month new-car loan. Her principal loan amount could be up to $23,000, and she would still have a monthly payment lower than $450.

When car companies are really keen on getting your business, they'll often advertise insanely low interest rates for new or certified preowned car loans. How many times have you seen 0% *Financing!* in big letters on your TV screen or blinking in the margins of a website? How often have you then squinted to read the teeny, tiny, black letters underneath that? Those little letters spell out that if you don't have a "top-tier" credit rating, as the financial people call it, you're not going to get that super-low interest rate. And I do mean best—0 percent financing often requires a score near 800 (most credit scores only go to 850, though Credit Karma has stretched it to 900).

Car ads sometimes offer zero-down deals. That means you aren't required to put a down payment on the car, though you will still be paying for taxes, titles, and fees at the dealership. The ideal down payment—the amount of cash you should have saved up for this huge purchase—is 20 percent of the total price. For a $25,000 car, that's a $5,000 down payment. For our example lady, that leaves a $20,000 car loan to finance, which, with a 6.4 percent interest rate, fits within her $450 a month budget. Hooray! (The average new car price in May 2015 was $33,560, so our example is on the less expensive—but perfectly doable—side of average.)

Another easy way to lower the annual percentage rate (APR) for a loan is to ask about automatic monthly payments.

Take The Wheel

You're probably using something like this for your cell phone or electric bill, but in case you aren't, auto payments are like direct deposit in reverse. If you agree to let the lender take your monthly car payment out of your account on a certain day every month, the lender will often drop the APR a bit. If you're not often overdrawn and you know you can keep the money in there every month, this will save you hundreds of dollars over the life of the loan. Having the payment directly drawn from your bank account also ensures that you're not late on a payment—which can get expensive with late fees and extra interest payments.

Part of that $5,000 down payment can come from the car you're driving right now, if you've got one. Trading in your current car to offset the down payment of a new car is especially helpful if you've already paid off the old car and own it free and clear, title in hand. Then whatever trade-in value you can squeeze out of the dealership can be applied to your new car. If you still owe on the old car, your trade-in value will have to be greater than the amount you owe in order for it to work as part of the down payment. Kelley Blue Book has a calculator that will spit out your particular vehicle's trade-in value (or resale value), which is handy for budgeting.

A couple of years ago, I had a ratty little red pickup truck that I wanted to get out of my driveway to make room for something with a back seat and all-wheel drive. The truck's trade-in value was $3,000; I still owed the bank about $2,000. The dealership agreed with my research that the truck was worth $3,000, so they paid off the bank loan I had on the truck and applied the remaining $1,000 to my

Creating Your Budget

new car. I could have sold the truck to pay off the loan and used the rest of the cash from the sale to make my down payment, which is what I've done in the past, but I wanted that thing out of my sight fast and with the least hassle. A week of seeing that truck, with its quirky, jerky transmission, parked at the curb with a *For Sale* sign in the window and sap from our walnut tree (not to mention squirrel poop) covering the windshield would have killed me.

If you don't have 20 percent to put down (and a lot of us don't), you'll have to borrow more money to buy a car. Any money you borrow, you have to pay interest on. The sales guy may let you get away with a 10 percent down payment on a $25,000 loan, but that's an extra $2,500 you'll be paying off over the life of the loan, plus another $195 in interest.

If you still owe money on your current car, some dealers and lenders will allow you to roll the balance into the new loan. Say you owe $5,000 on your current car, and the new one will cost you $20,000. They'll offer to write the loan for $25,000. Do not take them up on this seemingly friendly offer. It's a recipe for financial disaster. Why on earth would you pay interest on a car that you no longer own?

If you are considering using your car for a car-sharing or ride-hailing company like Uber or Lyft—which can be a great way to make extra money to make your car payment—make sure you tell any potential lender. Some classify car loans for those purposes as business loans, and the process of getting the loan might be more involved. If you're caught being untruthful with your lender, they can immediately

Take The Wheel

call the loan due and repossess the car if you can't immediately pay off the balance. You'll see something similar going on with insurance and ride-hailing companies in the next section too.

Budgeting for Insurance, Sort Of

You can pay your annual insurance premium every month, every six months, or in its entirety once a year, but you are going to pay it. It's required. You can get the minimum or the maximum coverage, and you can set your deductible really low or really high, but you have to have insurance. You'll be glad you have that magical little card one day, no matter who rams into whom.

How much you'll pay depends on so many factors, it's nearly impossible to list them all. Here are a few:

- Make, model, and year of the car
- Age of the driver
- Gender of the driver
- Location where the car will be driven
- Repairability
- Length of your commute
- Loss history statistics
- Deductible
- Length of relationship with the insurance company

Up until the late 1990s, the first four things on this list (plus the amount of the deductible) were really all that went into calculating the cost of any insurance policy for

Take The Wheel

a car. But just as consumers have tons of high-tech tools for shopping, insurance companies have tons of high-tech tools for compiling statistics on just about anything. With more data come more precise insurance rates.

Take repairability. Some cars are more easily repaired than others, as indicated by the mounds of data collected by insurance agencies. A car with easy-to-find parts and an easy-to-access structure is going to be cheaper to fix and therefore cheaper to insure. The now-defunct Saturn company, for example, built its vehicles with ease of repairability factored into the design and engineering.

When an insurance company has to pay out money on a claim, it counts that as a loss. A car with a lot of claims in its loss history is going to cost more to insure; likewise, a customer who has filed a lot of claims in the past is likely going to pay more.

In case you were considering it, jumping around between insurance companies isn't going to help you cover your tracks, Madame Fender-Bender. Nor will it get you a better deal in the long run. If you stick with one insurance company for a while and you're a decent driver without a lot of claims, you'll be able to build up accident-free credits, or discounts, on your insurance.

We've all heard the word *deductible*, but let's just take a moment to make sure we know what it means. This is the cash that you have to come up with to pay for any repairs before your insurance kicks in. A higher deductible—say, $1,000 versus $500—gets you a cheaper insurance rate. It also means that you'll have to pay a thousand bucks in a calendar year out of your pocket before you ever see a dime

Budgeting for Insurance, Sort Of

from your insurance company. The lower $500 deductible means less cash out of pocket when someone backs into your car in a parking lot, but it also means paying more overall for your insurance each year.

There are basically two ways to go with the deductible. If you're the kind of girl who keeps an emergency savings account for real emergencies, then the higher deductible is for you. Car repairs count as emergencies, without question. Shoe sales do not. If money flows through your hands like water, you might want the safety of paying a little more for the premium to avoid having to come up with a bigger wad of cash after an accident.

If you're planning on using your car to make some extra money as a driver for a ride-hailing service like Uber or Lyft, make sure your insurance policy covers that. Many basic and perfectly normal insurance plans not only don't include language that would protect you and your passenger, they will include fine print specifically forbidding you from driving a paying passenger around. If you get in an accident with a fare in the back seat, you could be left high and dry by your insurance company. Insurance is lagging behind the technology and culture on this front, so find a policy that covers ride hailing and car sharing if you're a new-economy kind of girl.

If you're a great driver with few accidents or tickets, you might be interested in the kind of insurance plan that's based on your exact driving habits. Your insurance company will send you a device that's basically a chunk of plastic that plugs into the OBD-II port just behind your steering wheel. It's no harder than plugging in a USB cord. The

Take The Wheel

OBD-II port allows the dongle to collect data from your car's central computer, things like speed, braking, steering, and distance traveled. If the data shows that you jam on the brakes pretty frequently, that's going to send a flag to the insurance company. It may mean that you're not paying attention to red lights or that you live in area where traffic patterns constantly cut you off. Both of those scenarios are more likely to result in an accident, and your insurer will adjust your rate accordingly. But if you follow the speed limit, ease the car to a stop, and don't swerve around like a maniac, your rate will reflect that.

It makes sense to pay an insurance rate that reflects your personal driving situation. But be aware that your insurance company is collecting data from your car, which might make some of the privacy minded among us a little squeamish. Very little personal data is actually being collected, and that data is likely aggregated with other data to make it more anonymous. There's no harm, though, in asking questions and reading the fine print on the privacy policy before plugging a dongle into your car and allowing yourself to be tracked.

One last thing on the insurance tip: young women do get lower insurance rates, thanks to our early maturation. But once we hit thirty, men and women are on an equal par, insurance-wise. (Income-wise, we're still trailing, at 79.6 cents on the male dollar in 2016. See the National Committee on Pay Equity for the latest disheartening numbers.)

Gas and Maintenance

The budget breaker you're going to run into all the damn time is the price of gas. Even when its price is low, as it is in 2017, it's still a cost you have to account for. Gas is more expensive in summer and sometimes cut with ethanol in winter to make it a little cheaper. That's how the gasoline game is played.

Your best bet in this mostly unavoidable game is to check out the US Department of Energy's handy web site, FuelEconomy.gov. This site is not sexy, unless you get off on numbers and charts (and admit it, some of you do), but it is a reliable way to compare the gasoline consumption of cars, trucks, minivans, and SUVs. You can even compare electric cars with gasoline cars, thanks to the MPGe (miles per gallon equivalent) calculation. Smaller cars with smaller engines get the best mileage, but they're often poky; heavier vehicles with eight cylinders or more get rotten gas mileage, but they can go fast or pull boats, which may be requirements for the car you buy.

That's the tradeoff you have to consider for your budget. If you're going to commute in heavy traffic on a boring freeway, a smaller car—maybe a turbocharged four-cylinder, maybe an all-electric vehicle—will serve you well. If you've got wiggle room in your budget, maybe spend your gas savings on a stereo that lets you hook up your phone using Apple CarPlay or Android Auto, or upgrade to a navigation system with real-time traffic to ease your hours of bumper-to-bumper crawling along the freeway. If you're a freelance web designer who works at home, first, high five, sister. Second, you might not care how much gas you burn those few times you trade your slippers for real shoes to venture away from your desk and climb behind the wheel.

You'll have to pay for maintenance less often than you'll have to pay for fuel, but it's still something to consider. If your car requires high-performance parts shipped from Europe, they'll be more expensive. If your car uses run-of-the-mill parts that come from a factory in Kentucky or Indiana, they'll probably be cheaper. Not all "foreign" cars are made in foreign countries, though, and not all "domestic" cars are built in the United States. Ask people who own cars built by the brand you're considering what their maintenance and repair bills are like. If their eyes mist over and they order another glass of wine before launching into a tale of expensive repairs and days at the dealership for an oil change, take note. Or you could just consult something like *Consumer Reports* or J.D. Power for reliability ratings and skip the tears and the wine tab.

Monthly budgeting for maintenance, insurance, and gas is going to be a special concern for women who own businesses that require driving. If you're hauling cleaning supplies, wedding cakes, or construction equipment over half the state, make sure your business can handle the related automotive expenses. And keep your receipts and a mileage log for tax time!

Wait! Do You Even Need a Car?

If you live in America, you live in the land of the freeway. This country is big and crisscrossed by a convenient (if boring) interstate system. The road trip and legend of the open road are our birthright. Everyone, it seems, has a car; some people have several.

But do you—just little old you—really need a car? As an individual, does the expense of a car even make sense for you? If you live fifty miles outside Great Falls, Montana, and you commute from the ranch to your job in town, you can stop reading and skip to the next chapter. You need a car. Probably a big one. Probably a pickup truck. Probably with a set of snow tires. Maybe a rig for a plow on the front.

The rest of you, though, the 82 percent of Americans who live in the city and have to deal with expensive parking garages or plows that pile snow on your car when it's parked at the curb in winter: you might not need a car.

The first choice for most of the carless is public transportation. Even if you don't live in New York City or Chicago, most cities have a decent bus system; the best have a train or subway system, too. A monthly pass is often roughly equivalent in dollars to an inexpensive monthly car insurance payment.

Take The Wheel

Depending on the meteorological and political climate where you live, bicycles are another great way to get around. Strap a couple of panniers on the back wheel, buy yourself some cool, brightly colored biking duds, get a cute helmet, and you're done. Bikes range from a couple hundred to a couple thousand bucks, and they save you not only a car payment but a gym membership, too. Bikes can often be used in conjunction with public transportation; if your city's got bike lanes, chances are the buses and trains have someplace for you to strap your bike up while you stay warm and dry on your way to work. Then you can bike home—all the exercise, none of the coworker-killing smell.

More and more cities also have car-sharing services like Zipcar or car2go. A monthly or per-use fee buys you time in a car—an hour, a day, a weekend, whatever you need. The company that owns the fleet takes care of insurance, the cost of gas, everything. Like everything else in your life, there's an app for every service that makes this whole thing super easy.

Zipcar stocks a variety of vehicles, from pickups to hybrids, so you're covered whether you want to run to the garden center or pick up your parents from the airport. It's a point-to-point system, meaning that you pick up a car from a Zipcar spot, drive it around for however long you want to, and return it to the same Zipcar spot. It's basically a short-term rental for members, and you pay for however much time you use.

Car2go began with a fleet of thousands of identical smart fortwo cars spread across the country, but they're switching to fleets of Mercedes-Benz vehicles. (Car2go,

Wait! Do You Even Need a Car?

Smart, and Mercedes are all owned by the Daimler Group.) It's a free-floating system, so members can hop into any car2go vehicle that's not in use, drive to their next thing, and leave the car in any legal parking space for the next person. If you get out and need to drive back in an hour or whatever, you take the next car2go vehicle you come across and do so.

Not owning a car may seem weird to an American mind, but in lots of urban areas it makes more sense than paying for parking, gas, insurance, and repairs. Plus, if you bike when you're not in your shared car, you'll have killer legs.

My friend Mel is a perfect example. She grew up in rural Idaho, where a car is absolutely required if you want to go farther than your front yard. But after living in bike-friendly Portland, Oregon, for a few years, she ditched her car completely. She was tired of paying for it, and she noted, "My car supported all my less-than-wise financial decisions, such as impulse shopping trips or driving to work and paying $10 a day for parking. I'm a lot less likely to make a late-night run for ice cream when I have to bike for it."

She spent years using her bike 95 percent of the time, including trips to the grocery store with a basket mounted on the back of her bike. She had Zipcar and car2go accounts that she used when she was too sick to ride or needed to buy something huge.

Eventually, after years of not having a car, she took up surfing. Driving 80 miles to the ocean with a surfboard did require a car with a rack, which most shared cars do not have. But she still commutes to work on her bike far more often than she drives.

Take The Wheel

If you're a candidate for a car-free life, Mel's got some good advice from the bike lane:

Plan ahead. Knowing all your options—i.e., the most convenient bus routes and what the fares are, the streets with bike lanes, and car-sharing options for emergencies—can make you feel more confident about not having your own car.

Consider easing into it. Go a week without using your car, then a month, until it feels natural. This took Mel a couple of years, but by the time she gave her car away (it was an ancient car, and she gave it to her sister), it didn't induce a panic attack. Not having a car becomes your routine.

Consider a bike. There are more and more resources for people using this form of transportation. "It's much quicker than walking, more independent than public transit, and can be really fun and adventurous," according to Mel.

Calculate how much owning a car costs per year. When you put a number on how much money you'll spend on a car payment, insurance, and maintenance in a year, you might find you want to use that money for more fun things. Mel budgets for public transit and occasional car sharing, and she says she's still saving thousands of dollars per year.

Part Two: Let's Go Shopping!

This is the fun part. Leave your budget behind for a couple of days and shop! Hit the internet, drive through some car lots, check out which cars catch your eye on your daily commute. Pay attention to commercials for once instead of tuning them out. You're just flirting with cars at this point, not marrying one.

Climbing the Decision Tree

No matter what the project is, everybody's got a strong suit. I am the queen of planning—comparing insurance rates, scouring the internet for the best loan rates, figuring out what kind of trade-in value I'm likely to get from whatever awful vehicle I'm desperate to ditch. The decision-making process is where I fall down. Maybe you can look at the available cars, trucks, and SUVs in your price range and home right in on your perfect vehicle. If so, I envy you. If you're like me, though, the number of decision points in the car-selection process is intimidating and makes you want to throw a blanket over your head and avoid the whole thing. By helping you, I'm hoping to help me. I'm selfish that way.

First, let's narrow down your field by figuring out what kind of car is going to suit your life. Later, we'll bring in the budget you've already created. Right now, get that dream bubble from the beginning of Part One back out, and it better not have that old Toyota Corolla in it. (A newer Corolla is fine.) You need to figure out what you need, want you want, and what drives you crazy in a car.

Back in the dark ages of car buying, before the internet, buyers would see ads on TV or check out their friends' cars and then go into the dealership to pick up brochures.

Take The Wheel

FUN FACT

There was an attempt at making the perfect one-size-fits-all car for women: the 1955 Dodge La Femme, an optional package for the Dodge Royal Lancer. We know how well one-size-fits-all T-shirts actually fit, right? That's how well this car went over, too. I am sure you've already guessed that it was a pink-and-white two-tone number. The official paint names were Heather Rose and Sapphire White, which I believe are names of two of the talented performers at the Dancin' Bare a couple of miles from my house. It also sported pink tapestry interior fabric, which apparently wore out faster than most upholstery, but that's fine. Women don't know anything about fabrics and durability. They'll never notice. It also came with a rain cape, rain hat, and umbrella, because women in the 1950s regularly melted into puddles of sugar. Buyers also got a pink leather purse with a compact mirror, lipstick, and a cigarette lighter and case. The La Femme lasted only two sad, pandering years before Dodge canned the idea altogether.

Brochures. When was the last time you saw a paper brochure? When was the last time you said the word brochure? Before the finale of *Buffy the Vampire Slayer* originally aired, I can almost guarantee it. Buyers also relied on the salesperson to tell them about the cars on the lot and the available features for each model. Now you can start the research process whenever the mood strikes you—from home, at work, even on the bus as long as your smartphone gets a signal—and tell the salesperson exactly what you'd

Climbing the Decision Tree

like when you find it. The salesperson of the twenty-first century may have some helpful guidance to offer, but you'll be far more knowledgeable than the consumer of yore the second you step through the door of the dealership.

In the course of poking about on the internet, take lists like "The Ten Best Cars for Women" with a grain of salt. A big grain. Big enough to throw at the guy who wrote the list and maybe leave a little mark. I've always been amazed that a whole entire sex, half the population of the country—nay, the world!—could be boiled down to an easy ten makes and models, according to these list-lovers. The entirety of womanhood cannot agree on ten lipsticks (color! texture! organic!), and those are cheap and easy to buy. Would anyone (except Ron Swanson on *Parks and Recreation*) ever write "The Ten Best Cars for Men" or even "The Ten Best Cars for Transgendered People"?

Besides matching purses and car interiors, there are a few things that are nonnegotiable for most people, regardless of their gender:

- **Kid friendliness.** If you'll be transporting little humans, you must have four doors to get them in and out of car seats and booster seats. Remember, you may have this car as long as eleven years, if the latest trends hold up. How old will the kids be during that time span? Do you plan on having more wee babies in the next few years? Or will they have grown into lanky, leggy teenagers?
- **The green factor.** Fuel economy and emissions are still important in an age of climate change, even if

the price of gasoline is low. Only you know if you're ready to go all electric, but there are so many hybrids, plug-in hybrids, and extended-range electrics available now, you won't feel restricted by choosing to go green.

• **Abilities in inclement weather.** Very few people ever take an SUV off-road, but lots of people go camping and skiing every year. A rear-wheel-drive sports car isn't going to cut it if you're one of those drivers; you'll want all-wheel drive and room for filthy, wet gear. Also, if you live in an area known for annual mudslides or snow measured in fathoms, you're going to want a car capable of dealing with those conditions in a pinch.

• **Automatic transmission.** Something like 90 percent of all cars sold in the United States have an automatic transmission. It's no longer true that manual transmissions get better gas mileage, so unless you're into learning to drive stick, it's okay to go with an automatic. It's not as fun, but it's okay.

Questions to Ask Yourself

There are hundreds of types of vehicles out there. Thousands, if you're also looking at used cars. The choices can seem infinite and overwhelming, but they're not. They're perfectly manageable as long as you ask yourself a few questions:

- **How much do I drive?** The average woman puts 11,500 miles or so on the odometer each year. Do you drive a lot for work? If so, you'll want a car with a great reliability record, good fuel economy, and a cushy interior. Urban car commuters are good candidates for electric vehicles. If you commute via bus or train every day and only use the car for weekend trips or monthly grocery shopping extravaganzas, you'll need more cargo space and can put less emphasis on fuel economy.
- **Is my driving mostly on the highway or mostly around town?** Highway driving means you're traveling at a constant speed, so your gas mileage will be better, even in an SUV. City driving has lots of stopping and starting, so a hybrid might be a better bet. Short trips on city streets could mean an all-electric car would work for you.

Take The Wheel

- **How do I use my car?** If you're often the only person in the vehicle, a small hatchback or sports car would work. If you've got kids, their stuff, and their friends, you're going to need lots of seats and space, as in an SUV or minivan. If you're a weekend warrior, you'll need space for tents, skis, coolers, maybe even a hitch and enough towing capacity for a boat.
- **How important is style?** Some people want a car that tells the world how sporty, sophisticated, or fun-loving they are. Some people don't care what their car looks like as long as they only have to do the bare minimum of maintenance. Figure out where you are on this scale and buy accordingly.
- **How important is safety?** Safety is paramount for some people. If it's your thing, make sure the cars you're looking at have lots of air bags, blind spot monitors, back-up cameras, maybe even advanced systems like automatic emergency braking—whatever it takes to make you feel comfortable in the car you buy. All twenty-first-century cars are required to have some safety systems (like advanced airbags and tire-pressure monitoring), so as long as you're buying a modern vehicle, you'll be covered to some degree.
- **Do I like to drive?** No one ever asks themselves this question, but they should. Some people love driving. They love taking the twisties at speed, or they love taking long drives to relax, or they love road trips and singing along with the radio. Other people think of it as a chore, like washing dishes. They'd rather do laundry than drive. When I am driving, I like driving.

Questions to Ask Yourself

I do not answer the phone in my car, I do not eat, I do not fish around in my purse for lipstick. I drive. But since I work at home and my daily commute is a forty-foot stroll across the back yard to my writing studio, I don't drive all that much. If you like to drive, horsepower, pound-feet of torque, and steering feel are going to matter to you. If you don't like to drive, you can ignore all these things, even though every glossy car magazine on the rack is going to treat them like the only things that matter. Focus instead on comfortable seats, safety features, and the ability to listen to calming podcasts while you commute.

Types of Vehicles

Now let's talk a bit about types of vehicles, which will make your research much easier.

• **Subcompacts** are tiny little cars that usually get great gas mileage and are a dream to parallel park. Sometimes these are called city cars, and the category includes the Fiat 500, Mini Cooper, and smart fortwo, which in the United States will only be available as an electric car going forward. Single ladies without kids and who don't drive on highways often like these cars.

• **Compacts** are small and fuel-friendly, but they've got a bit more presence than subcompacts. The Honda Fit and Nissan Versa are two popular compacts. These are for the woman who would rather not drive but has to, and they're cheap enough that you can add bells and whistles to the interior, like navigation and voice command systems or heated leather seats.

• **Sedans** have four doors and plenty of room. These range from stalwart family sedans like the Toyota Corolla and Subaru Legacy to upscale sedans like a BMW 5 Series. If you've got some serious swag in your bag, luxury sedans like the Rolls-Royce Phantom are out there, too. Sedans are great for families, especially if the kids are young now but will need some knee room as they grow. Sedans also offer the easiest in and out if you or someone who rides with you has mobility issues.

• **Coupes** are two-door cars and usually have an air of sportiness, with an engine tuned for performance and a lighter weight. The Ford Focus and Audi TT are both coupes, as is the Jaguar XK. Most of these fall into the fun and funky category, with fans in both the pre-kid twenty-something and post-kid empty-nester camps.

• **Convertibles** are available at nearly every price point, from the Mazda MX-5 Miata to the Mercedes-Benz E550 and beyond. Roadsters are cars with open tops and often stripped-down interiors to save weight for faster driving, like the Nissan 370Z. And T-tops, or targa roofs, have panels that can be popped out and stowed in the trunk, like the classic Porsche 911 Targa. Fair-weather women in the Sun Belt go gaga for drop-tops; everywhere else, these are usually summer cars that share garage space with an SUV or all-wheel-drive car for winter use.

• **Hatchbacks,** sometimes called three-doors or five-doors, can vary in size, but instead of a trunk, they all have a big liftgate in the back to access the rear cargo area, like in the Volkswagen Golf or the Mazda3. The "hot hatch" is usually a trim level that packs a lot of horsepower under that small hood. The Ford Focus

Types of Vehicles

RS, with 350 hp, counts, as do the VW Golf R and the Honda Civic Type R. Hatchbacks are great cars for spur-of-the-moment road trippers, with plenty of space for stuff and good gas mileage.

• **Station wagons** do the hatchbacks one better by having a huge cargo area behind the rear seats. The Audi A4 allroad and Subaru Outback are two of the vehicles in this category, which is sometimes blended with the crossover category. People who love station wagons *love* them. They've got space and a history of sportiness going back to the 1970s. If you want to rock the new retro, a wagon is it.

• **Minivans** have room for as many as seven people and at least one sliding rear door, plus cargo space and, lately, tons of amenities for families, like DVD screens, big storage bins, and built-in vacuum cleaners. The Chrysler Pacifica is now available as a plug-in hybrid minivan, and the Honda Odyssey and Toyota Sienna minivans have been around forever and constantly improved. The upside to a minivan is that the driver gets all the goodies. Minivans are loaded with standard features like heated seats, multizone temperature control, cameras and mirrors and sensors and all kinds of things to keep Mom happy as long as she has to drive this monster. Some models even have a small microphone near the driver that can broadcast all the way to the third row.

• **Pickup trucks** have a cab and a bed, and the size can vary hugely, from the little Ford Ranger to the mighty Toyota Tundra, which pulled the space shuttle

Take The Wheel

Endeavor through Los Angeles in 2012. Fans of country music love trucks, but so do new homeowners who find themselves at the home improvement store every goddamn weekend, or avid gardeners, or people with jobs and businesses that actually require a truck bed. Women construction workers and ranchers, we salute you.

• **SUVs,** or sport-utility vehicles, can haul boats and grade-school soccer teams, and they often have all-wheel or four-wheel drive for snow or mud. Land Rover and Jeep kind of rule this territory, especially if you actually go off-road. There is an SUV for just about everyone, from a small four-seater to a large seven-seater and from a gas sipper to a gas guzzler. Drivers of SUVs come in two basic types: the woman who wears her CamelBak and hiking gear everywhere, even to dinner, and the woman who wears her mini Coach bag and Pilates gear everywhere, even to the mall. One is usually found parking her SUV at trailheads, the other at the mall. One has filthy fingernails, one has totally fab fingernails. Sort yourselves accordingly.

• **Crossovers,** or CUVs, are usually smaller than SUVs but sportier-looking than station wagons, and they have more high-tech gadgets. They're also less likely to have true four-wheel drive with a locking differential, if you're into that kind of thing. The Ford Flex and Chevy Traverse are both crossovers. This category has ballooned in the last few years, as these vehicles are versatile enough for in-town

Types of Vehicles

maneuvering and a weekend of car camping. Crossovers ride the line between station wagons and SUVs, and so do the usually very practical women who buy them.

Technology

Contrary to what you might think, women generally *lurve* technology and gadgets in their cars, especially if they make life easier. There are very practical technologies, like minivans with second- and third-row seats that fold flat at the push of a button or SUVs with a hands-free liftgate.

Cars are becoming computers on wheels, and we're in a transition time between cars with carburetors and brakes you had to pump and shared autonomous pod cars. We've quickly adopted smartphone habits, and we're loathe to give them up just because we're driving. That's led to two types of tech: infotainment and ADAS.

Infotainment is a horrible word that refers to everything in the center console, whether it's a 5-inch screen with buttons or a 17-inch Tesla touchscreen. Navigation, satellite radio, and the ability to connect to your phone via Bluetooth are pretty standard infotainment features, though they are not standard on every car. You might need to pay extra or upgrade the trim level to get the tech you want. Since what we really want is to use our phones in the car, more manufacturers are including Apple CarPlay and Android Auto with their own infotainment systems. That means you can plug your iPhone or Android phone into the system and use a few preapproved apps, like Spotify, voice-to-text, and navigation right from your phone with a familiar interface.

ADAS stands for advanced driver assistance systems. A year ago, I talked to some auto manufacturers' representatives about ADAS, and it was a term they'd never heard or weren't using outside the engineering departments. Now everyone uses it. ADAS encompasses the first steps toward autonomous driving. This includes radar-based cruise control that locks onto the bumper of the car ahead of you and keeps you a set distance from that car. Lane keep assist technology lets you know when you've drifted over the line. Parking sensors help you parallel park, and some cars that you can buy today will just park for you, including Teslas, Jaguars, and Volvos. Two ADAS technologies, rear-view cameras and automatic emergency braking, will be required in all new vehicles as of 2018 and 2022, respectively.

While we're talking technology, let's talk about autonomous vehicles since everyone else is. The truth is, they're a long way off for most people. Cars with ever cleverer ADAS will be available, like, tomorrow. But a driver will be required. The systems that are being developed for personal vehicles now will alert you if your hands have been off the wheel for a while, or the car might even pull safely to the side of the road if it detects that you aren't able to drive. That's amazing, but it isn't fully autonomous.

Fully autonomous cars driven by robots—no steering wheel or accelerator pedal required—will first be used in limited cases. For example, autonomous shuttles are being

Technology

used at Gatwick Airport in London. They have limited routes and limited interactions with other vehicles. There are only so many places they can go, and they go there slowly. It's a pilot program that allows researchers to gather data on both the autonomous vehicle and on the reactions of riders. It's good practice for an autonomous vehicle future for the robots and the humans both.

Other Considerations

Pretty much any vehicle on the road with a model year later than about 2010 will be built to a high quality and have few issues. Many cars' computer systems keep tabs on your engine and driving habits to recommend things like oil changes and tire rotations when you need them. Reliability in a new car is going to be pretty good, unless you're getting a temperamental beast like a Ferrari, and really, even they've improved. So you can take the reliability question off the table if you want to eliminate a decision factor.

Design, inside and out, counts. Americans overall rack up an average 15,000 miles each year in their cars, so you'd better like what you see every time you see it in the driveway and every time you sit in the driver's seat. It's a matter of taste and of practicality. Will it fit in your garage? Can you park it in that tiny space at your office? You haven't reached the test-drive stage yet, but you'll get a gut feeling from looking at pictures on the internet and checking out cars on the street.

Make a list of however many cars catch your eye for any reason at all. Maybe it's ten. Maybe it's thirty-five. Whatever. When you've got a list of your dream cars (reliability and precise price are not factors here), do what your eye doctor does when he's fitting you for new lenses.

Take The Wheel

Pick two cars from your list, bring them both up on the web, and ask yourself, "Which is better, this one...or this one?" Eliminate the loser. Repeat until you have no more than a half-dozen favorites on the list.

Ta-da! Seriously researching five or six cars is far easier than the imposing task of pondering every car under the sun. If you are a nerd like me, you will make a spreadsheet now with the models, their pros and cons, their engine sizes and fuel economy, their cost, etc. If you are a normal human, you'll use a sticky note or a note-taking app to remember which models you like.

Back to the Budget

This is where your budget from Part One comes in. You might have a BMW 7 Series on your list, a heavy-hitting luxury sedan with an engine to satisfy your inner Danica Patrick. Spendy stuff if you buy a new one. But what if you get a used one? What kind of interest rate might your bank give you? What kind of monthly payment could you expect? It might not be so ridiculous after all.

If you've got a tiny budget that rules out new cars completely, something less than $15,000, there are still lots of great used cars out there, probably even cars on your list. Check U.S. News & World Report's used car ratings, Autotrader, and your local newspaper's classifieds section (probably online) to see what's available. You might have to settle for higher miles or an older car, but you'll be surprised what you can find that's both in your budget and close to something on your list of favorites.

If You Decide You Want New

Most of us eventually take the plunge and buy a brand-new car that has never been driven but for the kind, gentle soul who delivered it to the dealer's lot, where we test-drive it and fall in love. To some women, after owning a string of used cars that made them wonder what in the hell the previous owner(s) did to cause whatever problem they're having to deal with themselves, the allure of an unspoiled new car is almost tangible.

There was a time when the quality of manufacturing varied between makes, but really, that's no longer the case. Cars built today are put together much better right off the factory floor than they were even at the end of the twentieth century. When you've narrowed down your list by needs and budget, you may find a couple of cars on there that you didn't expect, which is great. There's no good reason to rule out a car because it's a Ford rather than a Chevy, or American rather than Japanese, or a newer brand rather than an older brand anymore. If it works for you, it'll be fine.

New cars come with far more standard equipment than ever before, from federally required safety systems like antilock braking systems (ABS) and advanced airbags to niceties like smartphone compatibility and push-button start. You can still find bare-bones cars with roll-up windows, but even these are going the way of MAC Viva Glam by Cyndi Lauper (man, I loved that lipstick), and they're really not much less expensive than models with electronic windows, locks, and mirrors, and maybe a USB port.

Almost every car on the market also comes in different trim levels, which means there are at least two, and sometimes more like five, variations of the same car. If you're looking at pickup trucks, with their long-bed/short-bed, crew-cab/extended-cab choices, there will be dozens of possible configurations. There will always be a regular version of the car and one that's got a few more things added, like heated seats, a bigger engine, or a nicer stereo. The base version of an expensive luxury car is still going to be pretty nice, mind you, and the nicer trim levels of an inexpensive commuter car are still going to be pretty basic.

The key is to know what you must have, what you'd like to have, what you can do without, and most importantly what you can afford. Drivers who deal with cold Minnesota mornings may have heated seats on the must-have list, no matter the cost. If so, check the trim levels to see if you can get heated seats plus some other nice stuff for a dollar amount that fits your budget. The Floridian who goes to great lengths to avoid hot seats, on the other hand, might go for a lower trim level—or spend the extra cash on a bumpin' stereo.

That's the fun stuff, but you can't ignore the practical stuff, like warranties. Some manufacturers, like Kia and Hyundai, offer 10-year, 10,000-mile warranties—the best in the biz. Most manufacturers offer warranties for the first three to five years, and the warranties cover only

If You Decide You Want New

the necessities, the things that make the car go, like engine parts and transmission. If the water pump or muffler falls off and skitters along the freeway, you're on your own, sister. Some warranties are better than others, so note this next to the model name on your short list in case you have to make a decision between two equally great-for-you cars.

You're likely doing your shopping online at this point, and maybe cruising past a couple of dealerships, stalking a few models. The danger here is forgetting about your budget. Do not forget about your budget. You can visit the Mercedes-Maybach website every day on your coffee break and dream about the included silver champagne flutes in the rear seat console, but for most of us, adequate cup holders are going to have to be enough.

If You Decide You Want Used

When we were younger, my friend Julius bought and sold used cars seemingly on a whim. He'd see a car parked in some guy's front yard—it was usually something like an old Datsun or Volvo—and stop to check it out. He was mechanically savvy, so he'd crawl all over the thing, and if it was drivable—hell, even salvageable—he'd start haggling with the guy right there in the tall grass that had grown up around the beast's fenders. He'd fix it, drive it, have a blast, sell it, and do it all again six months later.

This is not how most people approach buying a used car. First of all, most of us are looking for reliable transportation that we don't have to crawl under or take to the mechanic once a month. Second of all, as women, we are often highly attuned to the creep factor, which many sellers of used cars possess. Whether it's on a used-car lot or in a Craigslist ad, there's something sketchy about the guy getting rid of a used car.

The thing is, you can often get great deals on fantastic used cars. The car that was only driven to church on Sundays by a little old woman who had all the maintenance done on time at the dealership does indeed exist. Or the sporty little low-mileage two-door that a couple has to get rid of now that they're having twins. Or the gas-guzzling

Take The Wheel

SUV that doesn't fit with the urbanite's lifestyle but suits your ski-bunny ways perfectly.

The absolute easiest way to buy a used car with fewer problems than most is to find a certified used-car program at the local dealership. If you know what you want (and you should, if you've got that handy list of half a dozen cars from earlier in this section), check out the certified used inventory online. Be aware, though, that *certified* means that the dealership has checked 147 things on the car, or 253 things, or whatever they advertise. You need to look for a specific mention of an extended warranty being included, how long that lasts, and what exactly it covers. It's not going to be as good as the original warranty, that's guaranteed. But many certified preowned (or CPO) programs offer little perks like 24-hour roadside assistance, a rental car if yours has to spend time in the shop, or three free months of satellite radio in addition to the warranty to sweeten the deal.

Most dealerships have pictures and information online for every car on the lot that day, so you can see what years and what kind of mileage they've got on hand. If you don't see what you want, check back later. If you've got your heart set on something specific, like a first-generation Toyota RAV4 EV, which is rare as hen's teeth because it was only sold in California for a little while, let the salesperson at the dealership know. She can keep an eye out for a used car in your price range.

Another cheap and easy way to get a used car is to buy one from a rental car fleet. Every rental car company has a mileage cutoff, something like 10,000 or 25,000 miles.

If You Decide You Want Used

When a car reaches that magic number, it gets sold to whoever would like it, sometimes at auction, sometimes to a private party. This is a great way to get a low-mileage car that may still be under warranty. The drawback here is the way people treat rental cars. Think of your own rental car history: the four-day cross-country trip at ninety miles an hour, the bottle of sunblock you spilled on the carpet during spring break, the time the baby projectile vomited between the airport and your mom's house. Or think about the shitty rental cars you've been stuck with. I've had one with ocean salt sprayed all along the fenders, a sure way to eat the paint off and corrode the undercarriage, and one where the seat was stuck all the way back and would not move any closer to the steering wheel. I'm only five-foot-five, and there were literally no other cars in the lot on a Friday night. I drove it 250 miles laid back like I had my mind on my money and my money on my mind.

When you're at this used-car browsing stage, you're looking first at the cars you like and second at the cars you can afford. The third thing you'll want to notice is the mileage. Some high-mileage cars have been taken care of better than some children, and some low-mileage cars have been thrashed within an inch of their lives. But as a rule, lower numbers on the odometer mean a longer life for the car.

There are a few numbers that can serve as guidelines. If the average American drives 15,000 miles a year, a car built in 2012 should have about 75,000 miles on it by 2017. If it has far fewer, that's great! But the seller probably knows it's great and will charge accordingly. If it has far more, it could mean the car was used heavily—or it could mean it was used for long trips at steady highway speeds, which isn't so bad.

Any car with more than 100,000 miles is questionable, especially if it's going to be your main mode of transportation and your boss cares what time you punch in each morning. I know, your dad tells stories of the truck he had with a quarter million miles on it, and your college boyfriend said that a Volvo with 150,000 miles has just been broken in. Bullshit in both cases. If you were the only owner from new and you took great care of the car, then these scenarios might hold water. But if you're buying used, you have no idea what kind of care and feeding the car got.

You may see ads for cars that have something like 100,000 miles on the car but only 20,000 on the engine. This means the engine under the hood is not the engine the car came with when it rolled off the factory floor. There are two pretty likely reasons for an engine swap. One is that the car is vintage, like a 1969 Chevy Camaro, and the engine wasn't holding up over the years. Putting a new engine in will make the car less collectible but way more drivable.

The other reason to put a new engine in a car is that the old one blew up. Maybe there was something wrong with it, or maybe the owner ignored the Check Oil light. If the car was built in the past ten years but it's got a new engine, be very wary. If the owner neglected the engine, the rest of the car is probably in pretty sorry shape too.

Unless the seller has maintenance receipts. That, according to Audra Fordin, is the magic key, and she would

If You Decide You Want Used

know. She's the owner of Great Bear Auto Repair & Auto Body Shop and founder of Women Auto Know. "I want to see records," she says. "I don't believe anybody." If two people are selling the exact same car but one car has low mileage and the other comes with a folder full of receipts, she'll take the car with the maintenance history every time.

If the owner doesn't have those receipts, you can at least get an idea of any major issues in the car's past. CarFax has been around long enough that it still has *fax* in its name, and it's earned a reputation for alerting potential owners to huge problems with a car. Every vehicle in the world has a VIN, or vehicle identification number. Give this unique number to CarFax, and it will tell you:

- If this car has been in any serious accidents, and if there was frame damage or airbag deployment.
- If it was flooded (lots of cars had this problem after Hurricane Katrina in 2005).
- If the odometer has been messed with.
- How many owners the car had, and if those owners were rental agencies.

Many dealerships offer CarFax reports for free, especially with a CPO vehicle. You'll often see links to a CarFax report on dealers' websites, including those that list through Autotrader and Cars.com. If you're buying from a private seller, it's not too much to ask that they provide a CarFax report. It's only about forty bucks, so if they won't buy it, you can do it yourself. Or you can see that for the red flag it probably is and walk on by.

Take The Wheel

Keep in mind, though, that CarFax is only as reliable as the people who report these problems. If a guy runs his own car into his own garage and has his friend at the shop straighten out the crunched fender for him, he's not going to report that to the police or an insurance company. If he never reports it, it won't show up in the CarFax report. Anything that does show up on a CarFax report is at least a negotiating point, if not a complete deal breaker.

Leasing a Car

If **a car** commercial comes on during *America's Next Top Model* and mentions a monthly payment, it's likely the lease payment, not a loan payment. The difference is, at the end of a loan, you own the car free and clear. At the end of a lease, you turn the car back in to the manufacturer.

Leasing a car is like leasing an apartment. There are agreements to sign and money to put down, usually a few thousand dollars. (Car commercials like to put the amount due at signing in teeny, tiny type under the huge numerals of the monthly payment or at the bottom of the screen.) There are lots of pages of agreements to sign, and they detail what you may and may not do, and what types of things will incur penalties at the end of the lease.

For example, in your apartment, if your cat claws the hell out of the pantry door because he knows the food is kept in there, you will be buying your landlord a new pantry door when you move out. It'll probably be above and beyond whatever pet deposit you put down, since that mostly covers the sixteen vacuum bags it will take the move-out cleaning crew to get all the cat hair out of the carpet. Likewise, leased vehicles often have restrictions on things like the number of miles you can drive while you have the car. If you go over the mileage (12,000 miles is typical), you'll be paying for the privilege.

The advantage often cited for leasing a vehicle is that you can easily swap out for a new car every three years or so. Hardly anyone does that, but maybe that's important to you. The real advantage is that leasing is almost always cheaper per month than buying, provided you have the money stashed away for the payment due the day you sign the lease and another wad of money for any fees they stick you with at the end of the lease. Did you really think the dealership would be nicer about fees than any landlord you've ever had?

Also, there's a culture of ownership in the United States that says owning your car, or your home, is better than leasing or renting either. After the economic fallout of 2008, many consumers took a hard look at that conventional wisdom to see if it had any bearing on their lives. Ownership doesn't carry the cultural cachet it once did with younger buyers, who pay monthly fees for streaming music and movies anyway. They're also more likely to take advantage of car sharing in urban areas.

Online Shopping

You're a savvy, twenty-first-century woman, so the next step is likely to be online shopping. Even if you're not savvy, the internet is still probably your next step, though you've probably poked around online already by this point.

The most obvious online starting point is the manufacturers' websites. You've got a Chevy Spark on your short list? Hit Chevrolet.com first. Every manufacturer has a web site with every new car available for the current model year. Often, they'll have links to their approved local dealerships, too, so you can see what's available right now on the lot. That's where you'll find the leasing and finance deals that apply to your area too. Not every deal is available in every zip code.

The beauty of these online sites is that you can try before you buy. Not that you can take a useful virtual test drive—what auto manufacturer in its right mind would program in its car's quirks?—but you can test-drive your budget. Here's where you'll really get into those trim levels. There's always a base level that has minimal standard equipment and a top level that has every goody possible crammed in. Often, there will be a couple of midlevel models with some of the goodies, but not all, at a price between the two extremes.

Take The Wheel

Manufacturers' web sites will allow you to play with the car of your dreams before you ever talk to a salesperson, so open a beer, crank up Spotify, and outfit yourself with a bright yellow Mini Cooper with a checkerboard roof. No one but your browser will know, and you never have to order the thing. Start with a trim level close to your budget, then add features you consider important (all-wheel drive or Bluetooth connectivity, maybe). The site will keep tabs on how much it would cost to order the car as you equip it.

This is a perfect way to find out what standard and optional features are available for the cars on your list. Maybe one car comes with air conditioning as standard equipment, while on another it's a $500 option. Is price or staying cool in an Arizona summer more important? What other features come with each car? Try swapping out features. If you forgo the leather seats, maybe you can afford the nav system. Open another beer and keep playing, but stop drinking before you hit any kind of Buy button. Late-night online car purchases are a terrible idea.

While you're on the site, check for incentives. These are usually breaks on the APR of a loan serviced by the manufacturer's financing arm, or they can be cash-back deals. Don't discount these incentives; they can bring the price of a mildly expensive car down within your comfort level. Some incentives, like excellent interest rates, are only available to buyers with a certain credit rating, so you'll want to check with the dealership to see if you're eligible for the incentive. In an ideal world, you'd decide on a car that's already within your budget and then apply incentives to be well within your comfort zone, but incentives

Online Shopping

can also bring a car just out of your budget's reach down to a price or monthly payment you can afford. Just don't let incentives dazzle you into buying more car than you can afford.

If you do find and configure the car of your dreams, most manufacturers' sites will usher you through some kind of hold or purchasing process through a local dealership. Don't make a $30,000 decision while you're drunk, but if you revisit your configured car the next morning and it still seems like a great, sober idea, then feel free to skip to the section in this book on test drives and pull the trigger, you decision-making machine.

Many times, if buyers think they've found the right car for the right price, they'll initiate contact with the dealership via chat or email. Women in particular like to start the conversation this way, as you can feel more comfortable and in control at this point in the process. You're always in control of your decision, but having an electronic barrier helps you practice for the face-to-face conversations that are pretty much inevitable later in the process.

Those of you looking for used cars aren't left out of this process. Plenty of dealerships put their used-car inventories online, and they keep them updated. If you know what you must have in a car, you can check these sites as often as you like to see if a car with your preferences comes in. Especially when shopping for a used car, if the must-haves are in place, the mileage is reasonable, and the price fits your budget, jump on the best opportunities you find online. If it's a funky color, can you live with it? If it's missing a cool-ass stereo system, can you put one

Take The Wheel

on your birthday wish list? Stalking a dealership or two online and then pouncing the minute the right car comes up is as satisfying as a lioness's successful hunt. Or so I imagine, not being a lion myself but feeling pretty badass when these things work out.

TrueCar

TrueCar is a company that has dealerships shaking in their shoes. Where sources like Kelley Blue Book and Edmunds.com tell you what other people in your area paid for a car similarly equipped to the one you want to buy, TrueCar gives you an estimate of what the dealer's cost is. After arming the buyer with this information, TrueCar hooks up the buyer and a dealership or four that will deliver a guaranteed price—they've got relationships with over four thousand dealerships in the United States.

Depending on the business laws in your state, you'll either be offered an "up-front price" or "guaranteed savings"—say, $2,000 off the manufacturer's suggested retail price (MSRP)—by the dealership that you find through TrueCar. If the deal goes through, TrueCar takes a couple hundred bucks from the dealership for introducing you to their sales lot. You shouldn't be charged anything for it.

A couple of warnings are in order for TrueCar users. First, as was pointed out in a *New York Times* article, Honda found that some of its shadier dealers were luring TrueCar researchers to the dealership with the car the customer wanted and then trying to get the customer to buy a more expensive vehicle or add expensive options to drive up the cost of the car—and the salesperson's commission.

Take The Wheel

My friend Marilyn had a brush with these dastardly practices when she used TrueCar to find the Ford Focus of her dreams. She accepted the dealership's offer and agreed to come in the next day to finalize the reams of paperwork that were still required. Little did she know, another couple had driven the car before she did and, while she was doing her own test drive, the other couple was completing the paperwork and buying Marilyn's car.

Though she hasn't practiced in decades, Marilyn is a trained lawyer, so she called them out on their shenanigans. With all her legal training, though, Marilyn knew she had a weak spot that wasn't going to help her in negotiations. "I'm embarrassed to admit we'd gotten somewhat stuck on the color, which was hard to find," Marilyn told me via email. The dealership promised to make it right—color and all. "Three attempts later, the dealership finally found and traded for the right car. At that point their focus was on pleasing [me]—not on making a profit."

But don't run screaming from TrueCar—it can be a handy tool in your internet research toolbox and can eliminate the nasty negotiating process. "I should add I was impressed to get a couple of calls from TrueCar while the searching process was underway to ask how things were progressing," Marilyn says. And the company sponsored a team that included driver Katherine Legge at the 2012 Indianapolis 500, so clearly they want women's business.

Craigslist

There was a time when, if you wanted to sell your car yourself, you'd fill out a form with one letter per box and send it in to the newspaper. If you wanted to buy a used car from a private party, you'd scour the classified ads for the car you were looking for at a price you could afford. This usually meant squinting at newspaper type and puzzling out cryptic descriptions like "5sp man pw pd pl" (that's five-speed manual transmission, power windows, power doors, power locks, by the way).

But that was before Craig and his amazing List. Nearly every city in America, and many cities around the globe, has a list dedicated to its location and the crazy things people want to sell. Or the things crazy people want to sell.

Buying a car from Craigslist is no different from the old classified ads. You scan (or search using the text boxes at the top of the web page) for the car or cars you want and can afford. It becomes a bit of an obsession until you find one or two that seem to fit the bill, despite the spelling errors and shaky camera-phone pictures.

I'll say it here, because your mom is going to say it as soon as you tell her that you're going to check out a car you found on Craigslist: that site is full of rapists/murders/losers luring in smart women/attractive girls/ridiculous

Take The Wheel

airheads like you with their pictures of shiny cars. (Choose which phrases your mom is most likely to use.) There are undoubtedly whack jobs using Craigslist; check out the CL forums if you're feeling steely.

There are also lots of legitimate, non-weird men and women like you who are looking to unload a car without dealing with a dealership. Basic tenets of safety apply:

- Check the car out in the daytime.
- Arrange to meet the seller somewhere public and busy, like a gas station or mall parking lot.
- Tell someone where you're going and what you're doing.
- Or take a friend, preferably a scary one, not necessarily a male.
- Test-drive the car, but don't let the seller lead you down dark alleys or dirt roads.

These rules apply no matter where you're test-driving a car, especially a used one, but Craigslist has a reputation for weirdos and flakes. Your mom won't call you every five minutes if you promise her that you'll follow those basic rules. She'll keep it to a much more reasonable fifteen-minute recurring check-in.

Apps

There are several businesses working to take the hassle and haggle out of buying cars, especially used cars. Carvana, Shift, Vroom, and other startups have recently come online to serve as the middle app between you and the seller. In some cases, you don't have to visit the dealership at all; the service will deliver the car to your door.

But it's a tricky business. One startup, Beepi, crashed and burned three years after it went live. Others have popped up, but none of them have really gained a solid footing in the used car market and turned a profit. They may be great solutions for time-crunched, negotiation-shy women, but they're popping up and burning out faster than this book can track. Maybe by the third edition of this book there will be a clear winner in the online used car business.

At the Dealership

Going to the dealership is no longer the sexist sleaze-fest it once was. Or it shouldn't be anyway. "Any consumer, woman or otherwise," says Annette Sykora, past chair of the National Automobile Dealers Association, "should go into a dealership expecting to be treated with respect, to have their questions answered, and to have a professional experience. And if they don't, then they should go somewhere where they do find that."

Sykora takes these things seriously. She's been in the business with her own dealerships in Texas since the early 1980s. "I loved the people, I loved the new cars, and I had the gasoline in my blood," thanks to her dad, who also owned dealerships. "This really was the business for me."

But thirty years ago, women were a rarity on the showroom floor. Sykora was the first for her company. "In those days, it was more about the men customers accepting a woman being there. Now, our consumers want to do business with people that respect and appreciate them. Even if they aren't dealing with a woman salesperson, the fact that they see a lot of women staff in our store is good; it's comforting. They see that there's a lot of women here in several positions and think, 'Surely they know how to do business with women.'"

Take The Wheel

Sykora says everyone who walks through the door anymore is an expert in the vehicles they're interested in. The challenge is for salespeople to make sure the buyers are getting what they need and not what they think they want. "With all of the information available to all consumers, regardless of gender or ethnicity, that in itself means the consumer is more informed. In dealing with more informed consumers, it's mandatory that dealerships and personnel be able to rise to that level to deal professionally with an informed consumer and serve informed consumers so they do feel respected and their knowledge is appreciated."

Many people, especially women, are relationship buyers, Sykora says. So by all means, establish a good, comfortable relationship with someone at the dealership and let him help you. Buyers are often reluctant to offer up too much information, which is understandable, especially with the horrid reputation car salesmen have. But if you can explain to the salesperson why you're interested in the car you've researched and what you'll be doing with the vehicle, he will be able to make sure you've matched up your needs with what the vehicle can offer.

"I understand being guarded," Sykora says, "but if you feel you have to stay on defense the entire time, you're probably not working with the right person or the right company. There may be someone different within that same company who's better for you."

This is a big-ticket purchase, and salespeople like Sykora appreciate that. "Women should remember that this is always in your control, it is your decision, and don't make a decision that you aren't comfortable making. Trust your instincts."

At the Dealership

Before you head out of the house to look at real cars on real lots or in real driveways, let's make sure all the confidence-boosting research is in place:

- You've got a target price for the car you plan to buy, plus or minus a thousand dollars or so.
- You've got an idea of what you can afford each month as a lease or loan payment.
- You've narrowed your choices down to a half-dozen at most (likely by now there are only about three vehicles you're seriously thinking about).
- You've looked at what's available, new and used, online. Maybe you've even done a drive-by at a dealership or two.
- You've put all this information together in a folder, either a physical one you carry with you or a virtual one you carry on your phone. Make sure you've got the CarFax and a couple of value estimates printed out or bookmarked. Kelley Blue Book is a standard, but websites like Edmunds.com have good numbers for comparison too.

Drive It Like You Own It

It's now time to take all this planning and put it into practice in the physical world. It's time to take a test drive.

The first instinct many women have is to bring along the husband/boyfriend/dad. The boys will mash the accelerator, stomp on the brakes, make up some shit about torque and lifters, spout some numbers they heard Jeremy Clarkson spout on *Top Gear*, and offer an opinion that in the end makes no difference. This is your car. You will drive it, probably every day, twice a day, for the next six and a half years. How does the acceleration feel to *you*? Are the brakes too squishy or too hard for *you*? You're going to pay for it, you're going to live with it, so you're going to test-drive it.

Here's what Sykora, with three decades of dealership experience under her Texan belt, has to say about that: "It's not necessary to bring a man along, but it is necessary to bring your confidence along."

Here's the other important thing about test-driving: you cannot do it wrong. There is no such thing as a test drive that is too long or too short (as long as you don't drive to Nunavut or something). Drive like you normally would, radio blasting or quiet, fast or slow. Don't let whoever is in the passenger seat trying to sell you the car tell you what to do or how to drive. If he wants to point out some helpful

Take The Wheel

or interesting feature, like a sunroof you might not have noticed, that is welcome information. If he wants you to take one turn around the block, or if he tells you there's some special way to do something completely normal, like putting the shifter into drive, smile politely and ignore him.

I've got one last piece of reassurance before I send you off to the car lot. You know as much about the car you want by now as just about anyone, outside of the guys (they really are mostly guys; yet another ratio to change) who designed it and built it. You've done your research and picked the cars you're interested in. You know which features are available and important to you. Not even salespeople know all of this stuff about every car on the lot, and unless your dad is a factory test driver for BMW and you are buying a BMW, you should trust your own research. Input from family and friends can be helpful, but there are a lot of opinions out there without a lot of foundation. You've got this. You're a smart lady.

Okay! On to the test drive!

Get the keys. If you're looking at a used car, you'll probably have set an appointment with the owner for the test drive, and he'll be waiting for you. If you're visiting a dealership, you can either go inside and tell a salesperson which model you'd like to test-drive or wander around the lot until someone approaches you.

Get in. And out. And in. When you've got the keys in your hand and you've made nice with the owner or salesperson, open the door and get into the driver's seat. Do it a couple of times, even if you feel silly. Do you plop into it, or glide? Is there a big step up, or a big fall down, to

Drive It Like You Own It

the seat? Is that comfortable for you? Does the door open wide enough, or so wide that you can't reach it once you're seated? Can you get in and out in a pencil skirt, if you're a pencil-skirt kind of girl?

Start 'er up. Either turn the key or press the Start button. What does it sound like? Do you like the sound? Let it idle a few seconds while you get used to the sound so you have a baseline. This warms up the engine, too.

Push buttons. Turn on the lights, the air conditioning, the heat, the radio, the turning signals, everything. Especially if it's a used car, watch the "'hello, good morning' lights," as Audra Fordin at Great Bear Auto calls them. The lights that flash on when you start the engine signal that the car is running through a system check. When they're all off, you're ready to drive. If any stay on, take note. That's a problem. Especially if it's the one that says "Check Engine."

Take it for a spin. Adjust the mirrors so you can see, and turn on the heat or A/C or whatever to make sure it works. Put the shifter into drive (or first, if it's a manual transmission) and head out. Take off slow and smooth to adjust to a new-to-you gas pedal; then press the brake while no one is behind you so you aren't surprised by its grippiness or lack thereof when you're in traffic.

Drive! This part should last at least twenty minutes. A quick trip around the block will not do, but tooling around the neighborhood for a bit is a good start while you get used to the controls. If there's a highway nearby, get on and off. How does it do merging into traffic? What are the blind spots like? Drive to a grocery store or mall or whatever's handy and park to see if it's easy enough or if you're going to cringe every time you swing into a space. Bonus points if you parallel park in a car completely unfamiliar to you.

Bring it back. After about a half hour, return the car to where you found it. But you're not done. This is when you give the interior a good going-over. While you're still in the driver's seat, look at what's in reach. Cup holders, climate controls, radio controls, nav system: how many of these things do you regularly fiddle with while driving? Can you reach them without taking your eyes off the road? If adults ride with you, sit in the back seat and make sure adults will fit.

This time, it's personal. We've all got at least one car quirk—the one thing we absolutely need our vehicle to do, the deal breaker. If kids ride with you, bring their car seats and see how they fit. If you snowboard, bring your board to make sure it fits in the cargo space. If you bake immense specialty cakes, bring a cardboard mockup to see how it sits on the floor of the vehicle for transport. If this is the van for your band, bring your biggest, gawkiest piece of equipment, like a drum kit or a couple of amps. You get the idea. (My car quirk? Dog-friendliness. Comfortable, safe, cleanable rear seats with a window that rolls down and a place to stash toys and towels. My dog has to be able to hop in and out without me lifting or cajoling him.)

Several years ago, my husband's beloved Volvo started leaking oil at about 250,000 miles. We were going to buy our first-ever brand-new car to replace it. We set a budget and picked a half-dozen cars to check out. (Confession: I made a spreadsheet of models he liked with stats and pros and cons. It was not received with the amazed gratitude I expected.) He decided in the research phase that he liked the Honda Element since he's tall and he carries a lot of stuff in boxes for work. So we went for a test drive at a dealership in the suburbs.

We picked the Element with the lower trim level that we could easily afford and took a quick test drive with the sales guy. While we were debating, the hubs got a call that he needed to attend a meeting in the city. The sales guy, seeing we were interested, kindly allowed us to take the Element to the meeting. Over the course of about an hour on highways and streets, in traffic and on open roads, we realized that the vehicle was missing some stuff my husband wanted to have, like a center console, a better stereo, and nicer upholstery. We brought the Element back and told the sales guy what we wanted. He suggested we take a spin in an Element with a higher trim level. It had every single thing the hubs had listed as missing in the basic edition, plus a couple of nice extras. For a little more money, but still inside our budget, the hubs got exactly the car he wanted.

With used cars, there are a few other considerations. Someone else has been driving this car for several thousand miles, and some weirdnesses are bound to develop. Checking the acceleration, engine noise, ease of shifting, and brakes is especially important. Many things are cheap and easy to fix—brake pads are something like twenty bucks and you could seriously change them yourself if you felt like it—but some things aren't. On your first test drive in a used car, go with your gut. If it seems fine to you, proceed. But if you're questioning it at all, move on to the next car on your list.

Take The Wheel

Because a used car has been around the block a few times, really give the interior and body a close inspection. Scratches in the paint aren't usually a big deal, unless it looks like the metal underneath is starting to rust. Look for dents or ripples or anything that seems like it's been shoddily repaired. Look for signs of water damage from floods, especially in the upholstery and carpets, where the smell will linger. Run a CarFax for the VIN to see if it's in the clear.

Ask the person selling the used car if you can take it to your mechanic for a look-see. "Before you take the keys, take it to a mechanic," says Fordin. The owner will probably say sure; if they don't, it's a deal breaker. The mechanic who checks out the car could be the guy you've been taking your cars to for years, or it could be your dad, if he's got some shade-tree mechanic skills. (See? He can be helpful. Just not during the test drive.) In any case, don't take it to the mechanic suggested by the seller, unless you happen to go to the same guy. The mechanic will know what to look for, but you want to make sure the oil has been changed regularly and the fluids, like brake fluid and coolant, aren't too low. If the brakes or tires are worn in strange ways, that can signal some aggressive or harmful driving in the car's past—or even frame damage.

In this case, you're probably ahead of the boys. LeaseTrader.com analyzed lease transfers in 2011 and found that two-thirds of women ordered third-party inspections when taking over someone else's lease. Only about half of men did the same. And younger women (ages twenty-one to thirty) were even savvier than their male counterparts, with nearly 80 percent requesting an inspection, while only 40 percent of younger men did. Women were also more likely to ask about safety performance, incident history, and how the vehicle works in certain situations, like accelerating onto a freeway or parking in a tight space. Men talked about performance and aesthetics.

Actually, Sheryl Connelly, manager of Global Consumer Trends and Futuring for Ford, says men and women want the same thing in a car, but they talk about it differently. In the above example, where women mentioned accelerating onto a freeway and men talked about performance, both buyers are talking about engine power, but the woman is using story and problem-solving terms, while the man is using technology and functionality to talk about the same aspect of a car. It's a little language quirk to be aware of while you talk to the salesperson or owner during the test drive, especially if you're talking to a guy.

Special Section:

Your Guide to Green(er) Cars

It's Pretty Easy Being Green

There are dozens of alternative-fuel vehicles out there right now, some of which are even available as used cars at this point. Let's take a quick tour of the choices:

- **Hybrid.** A gasoline-electric hybrid, like the Toyota Prius or Ford C-Max Hybrid, has a gasoline engine plus an electric motor. Some hybrids can run on electricity only for a bit, while some only use the two systems together at the same time.
- **Plug-In Hybrid Electric Vehicle (PHEV).** This is another gasoline-electric hybrid, but the batteries can be recharged by plugging them in as well as through regenerative braking and the like. The Chrysler Pacifica PHEV works this way.
- **Extended-Range Electric Vehicle.** This car, like the Chevy Volt, mostly runs on electricity and plugs into the wall to recharge, but it also has a small gasoline-powered motor as backup for long trips.
- **Electric Vehicle (EV).** This is all electric all the time, like the Nissan Leaf and Tesla Model S. No emissions and no gasoline mean it must be plugged in to recharge.
- **Clean Diesel.** Several Mercedes-Benz, Jeep, and Land Rover vehicles are available with the latest,

cleanest diesel technology, which gets highway mileage well above 40 mpg. But the Volkswagen emissions-cheating scandal of 2015 put a big damper on diesel.

• **Hydrogen.** There are very few of these on the road, like the Honda Clarity. It's basically an electric car whose batteries can be recharged by refiling a tank with liquid hydrogen instead of being plugged in.

There's a good chance, with so many of these cars on the market, that one of them landed on your short list. Let's dig deeper into each technology to find out if it's right for you.

At the dawn of the automotive age, people who could afford cars had lots of choices for fuels. There were gasoline-powered cars, electric cars, steam-powered cars, diesel cars, and even cars that ran on wood chips. They battled it out for a while, and some of these technologies never went away, but there was one clear winner.

Gasoline.

For about a hundred years, gasoline reigned as king of the road, with diesel working as its long-haul prince. Electric cars would pop up every once in a while, usually during times of gasoline crisis, but they never took off.

Then came the Tesla Model S. Many manufacturers were working on electrified vehicles in the early years of the twenty-first century, including Tesla and its initial all-electric Roadster. But when the Model S debuted in 2012, fanboys went bananas and major manufacturers had to follow suit. It was a pure electric EV with a range more than twice that of any other electric car on the road, it was high-tech, it looked good, and it was expensive. People ate it up faster than the company could produce them.

About the same time, the Nissan Leaf debuted, with a funkier shape and half the range. It sold well and was available in all fifty states, unlike some EVs. It swapped the top-selling EV spot with the Model S for several years as other manufacturers rolled out their own electric vehicles, like the Fiat 500e, Kia Soul EV, Chevy Spark EV, and a dozen others. PHEVs gained ground as a way to dip a toe into electrified driving without range anxiety, and range-extended EVs went even further—literally—by adding a tiny gasoline engine as a generator to keep the batteries charged. In the case of the Hyundai Ioniq PHEV, that's a total of 650 miles or more on a full tank and charge.

With all of these new powertrain technologies becoming more available outside California, more people are asking more practical questions. Nothing trumps your budget and a test drive, but this quick guide can help you narrow down what is now a wide field of alt-fuel choices.

What Is a Hybrid?

It **may surprise** you—or it may not, given the ubiquity of the Toyota Prius—to know that hybrids have been on sale in the United States since 1999. I'm sure when Prince wrote about partying like it was 1999, he never imagined he would do it using an electric-gasoline hybrid system. He was, of course, imagining little red Corvettes. I didn't have to tell you that.

Everyone has heard of hybrids by now, and most people know that they involve electricity. But even a decade later, these cars still have an aura of mystery. What exactly is going on under that hood?

Well, there's the first sticking point. It's only partly going on under the hood. Like many of us, hybrids got it going on in the trunk too. Hybrids have two sources of power: a gasoline-powered engine and an electric-powered motor. The engine is a combustion engine like the engines found in most vehicles on the road. Hybrid engines are engineered to save fuel in a way that sacrifices power at low speeds. But that's okay! Low speeds are where the motor kicks ass.

Electric motors have "all torque, all the time," as the electric car nerds like to put it. Torque is that awesome feeling of being thrown back in your seat when you stomp on the accelerator. A combustion engine takes a couple of seconds to reach maximum torque. In an electric motor, that happens nearly instantaneously when you hit the accelerator, like flicking a light switch. The problem for electric motors is that it's hard for them to keep up that kind of ass kicking. They run out of juice.

In a hybrid like the Prius, these two power sources, like ebony and ivory, work together in perfect harmony. I swear the '80s music references are not intentional, but there they are. You can drive the car up to a certain speed, say 40 mph or so depending on the car, for a few miles if you're careful, before the gasoline engine starts up and takes over. Then the motor just helps out a little while the engine does most of the work.

In some older styles of hybrids, the motor and engine always worked together at the same time. You couldn't drive these cars on electric power only, but the motor did help the engine with both torque and fuel savings.

There's no plug required in a normal hybrid. Like other electrified cars, hybrids have regenerative brakes, which means that they can capture the energy lost in the effort to stop the car and channel it back to the batteries. That energy is usually lost as heat that radiates out into the air, but this braking system is able to hold onto and use it before it has a chance to escape.

Who Gets the Biggest Bang for This Buck?

Since the motor takes on an assisting role at highway speeds, leaving the 75-mph, horsepower-heavy work to the gasoline engine, hybrids get better mileage in town than on

What Is a Hybrid?

> ### FUN FACT
>
> The first hybrid was invented probably a century before you think it was. Dr. Ferdinand Porsche, "Ferry" to his friends, invented the first gasoline-electric hybrid vehicle in 1901, before there was even a Porsche company to claim it. Dr. Porsche developed it during his first job as a young man with Jacob Lohner & Co. in Austria. It took over a hundred years for the Porsche company to get back on that hybrid bandwagon with the Cayenne SUV.

the highway. This seems counterintuitive to anyone born before the 1990s, much like my penchant for referencing '80s pop songs, but check out the Environmental Protection Agency (EPA) ratings for hybrids and you'll see the mileage distinction. You can find those ratings at FuelEconomy.gov or on any window sticker on the lot.

These cars not only work well for commuting city types, they also fill a hole in the environmental hearts of American heartlanders. There are lots of people in the middle of the country who would love to have a tiny electric car that runs on butterfly kisses and emits only rainbows, but their morning commutes involve long stretches on lonely highways in giant, empty states when the temperature is thirty below. They may love the earth, but they are not stupid. They are practical. A hybrid can be an easy compromise for those folks.

A hybrid is not going to get early adopters' motors running. If you have ever waited in line for an iPhone, or if you are a serial beta tester for apps, a hybrid is not going to be nearly exciting enough for you. However, if you're still unsure about all this electric car folderol, a hybrid is a stable, proven technology with millions of miles on all those odometers since 1999. Maintenance records are available, used vehicles are out there, and the price of new vehicles is no longer so far above a nonhybrid version that you might as well buy two cars.

Is It Really Green?

Hybrids are light green, like a Granny Smith apple—they're both easy to find, easy to like, and versatile. You can eat them out of hand or put them in a pie. Whether it's a full hybrid that can run on battery power for a bit or a mild hybrid that gets a boost from the motor, these cars usually get better mileage than a gasoline-only vehicle.

What Is a Plug-In Hybrid?

If a hybrid is dipping a toe in alternative fuels, a plug-in hybrid electric vehicle (PHEV) is rolling up your jeans and wading in to your knees. These are hybrids that recharge their batteries by plugging into a wall in addition to using regenerative brakes. They also have that trusty gasoline engine on board.

Plug-in hybrids have bigger battery packs that can store more energy—way more than you could capture with just the brakes. Plugging the car in overnight will give you an electric-only range that might get you to work and back the next day. Most PHEVs can travel 20–30 miles using electricity only.

These cars all have a gasoline engine on board to alleviate range anxiety—the fear that the batteries don't have enough juice to get you where you're going, which might leave you stranded alone on the side of the road at midnight in a desolate, moonless landscape ripe for murderous rapists. Anyway, you won't have to worry about that because plug-in hybrids have an engine. How they use that engine varies, though. Some use it just the way a regular hybrid does—when you ask your car to go a little faster or a little farther, like passing on the highway or taking a road trip, the engine kicks in and mostly does all the work.

Take The Wheel

But the engines in some plug-in hybrids never turn the wheels. Sometimes these are called range-extended vehicles, though the US Department of Energy classifies them as PHEVs. Their engines act as on-board generators for the batteries. You can drive a few dozen miles in a Chevrolet Volt on the power from your plug, but if you drive farther, the generator engine starts cranking out power and storing it in the batteries, so your electric motor can keep turning the wheels. If all you do is commute ten miles to work and ten miles home with an overnight plug-in, the gasoline engine might never fire up.

While a PHEV can recharge at any outlet, it will recharge quite a bit faster at a 220-volt outlet than at the more usual 110-volt outlet. There is a gasoline engine to keep you rolling, though, so whether you want to install a higher voltage outlet is really up to you. The 220-volt is the same kind of outlet your dryer uses, which is not all that special, but you probably don't have an extra one in your garage.

Who Gets the Biggest Bang for This Buck?

Like the hybrid powertrain of the 2000s, a plug-in hybrid gets its best fuel economy in town, where the electric motor can do most of the work. Once you get up to highway speeds and distances, the gasoline engine will start to help out, either directly or as a generator.

Compared to a conventional combustion engine, though, these souped-up hybrids are gas sippers. Plug-in hybrids work really well for one-car households, whether that's because there's only one adult who drives, or because you share a car, or because you both bike to work but occasionally need a car for groceries or trips to IKEA. Plug-in hybrids tend to be substantial vehicles rather than small cars, so they usually have four doors and room for kids in the back.

Having that backup engine gives buyers wading in the green-car marketplace a measure of security. No being stranded in a moonless landscape ripe for murderous rapists for you, plug-in hybrid owner! But the technology is still pretty expensive, so make sure that you'll be able to maximize the electric-only miles in order to justify the extra dollars.

Is It Really Green?

Here's a revelation: a plug-in hybrid is slightly more eco-friendly than a plain old hybrid and not as green as an electric-only car. Since that is pretty obvious, here's a quick look at the numbers so you can see for yourself what each type of car on the electric spectrum consumes and emits.

The easiest and most basic data to compare comes, yet again, from the EPA. The Toyota Prius Prime, Chrysler Pacifica Plug-In Hybrid, and Chevy Volt are representative of what a plug-in hybrid can do. Each of them emits 100–150 grams of carbon dioxide per mile or less. That's about a quarter of the average passenger car, which emits 411 grams per mile.

And that's if you drive it according to the boring old Environmental Protection Agency estimates. Owners of plug-in hybrids know all the tricks for eking out every electric mile, from charging every time they park to changing their commute routes to maximizing the downhills. Sites like VoltStats.net show what the dedicated plug-in hybrid owner can do. This site is devoted to the Chevy Volt, and users are regularly racking up more than a thousand miles per gallon.

On the driving side, plug-in hybrids are as green as you make them. You can use hypermiling tricks and charge during your utility's off-peak hours to maximize the green effects of the car and save money, or you can just drive it like you would any car and still get better mileage than you would from a car with only a gasoline engine.

What Is an Electric Vehicle?

There are two kinds of people in this world: those who would make great electric car owners, and those who would rip out their hair and scream like a banshee if they had to drive an electric car. And the dividing line isn't what you might think.

It doesn't take an engineering degree or a pair of homemade hemp pants to drive an electric car. It doesn't even take the stereotypical male early adopter, with his Zuckerberg hoodie and his crush on Siri. When the Nissan Leaf came out in 2011, for example, only 10–15 percent of buyers were women, according to the *Detroit News*. By early 2013, not even two full years later, women accounted for 25–30 percent of new Leaf buyers.

For many people in twenty-first century America, it doesn't take a sacrifice or a second thought to buy and drive an EV. If you have a regular commute that's shorter than about twenty-five miles one way, especially if it's a relatively flat route, then you're golden. Any emissions-free battery electric vehicle (BEV) can be your ticket to green-car good karma. Range and power in modern electric vehicles have improved so greatly that for most drivers, the only difference you'd notice is that the car is damn quiet.

Take The Wheel

> **FUN FACT**
>
> Electric cars were considered woman-appropriate vehicles when they were first introduced in the early 1900s. Not many people know that at the dawn of the automotive age, around the turn of the last century, cars were pretty much divided into three camps: gasoline, electric, and steam power. In the urban centers of the Northeast, they were around in roughly equal numbers, though they were all outnumbered by horses.
>
> Electric cars were considered to be best for women drivers, as they were quiet, they didn't smell, and they didn't require messy refueling. Electric cars also had fewer parts to break (all of which is still true). No less an authority than Henry Ford bought an electric car, which the Ford Motor Company did not manufacture at the time, for his wife.

Any EV should get about 100 miles on a full charge. Teslas get far more than that, with EPA range ratings well above 200 miles. And the Chevy Bolt EV joins Tesla in having a range comfortably over 200 miles.

If you want an EV that looks like it came from the future, the Nissan Leaf can meet that need. If you want luxury and prestige, Tesla is on it. If you want practicality, the Bolt is kind of boring but very useful. If you want a car that blends in, the VW e-Golf looks like every other Golf. There's an EV for everyone, really. If you can find it.

The trouble with EVs isn't their range or their usability; it's being able to find one at a dealership. California has every

What Is an Electric Vehicle?

EV available. Oregon, Washington, New York, and a couple of other states have several. In the middle of the country, you can get things like the Kia Soul EV, but there isn't likely to be one on the lot, charged up and ready for a test drive. You have to order it. Manufacturers are doing a terrible job of promoting EVs outside California, and dealerships are doing a terrible job of selling them. You have to sell yourself on the idea; no one is going to help you.

If you're on the fence, here's my best argument for EVs: because of the torque, they make city driving way more fun than in a regular car. You can mash the pedal at every red light and race to the next one—no gasoline used, no emissions, and hardly any sound unless you manage to chirp the tires, which would be awesome.

Who Gets the Biggest Bang for This Buck?

According to 2010 US Census data, more than 80 percent of Americans live in urban areas. And it takes nearly two-thirds of us less than half an hour to get to work. That puts a lot of people in the sweet spot for electric car ownership, whether they know it or not. For a lot of families, one EV and one gasoline vehicle make sense. One parent commutes in the EV and one in the "regular" car. In many cases, the gasoline-powered car is an SUV or minivan, something the whole family can pile into for weekend camping trips or visits to Grandma's for the holidays. The EV helps offset the emissions and fuel cost of the bigger vehicle.

Like your phone, the batteries do have to be charged, and for now that's best done overnight at a 220-volt in-home charger. If you're lucky, your employer or parking garage will have designated charging spaces for a midday top-off. Often dealerships and the local utility will have some kind of partnership or financing deal for installing the charger properly and up to code, which is worth the expense if it's going to power the car you use to commute to work every day.

Some cars are able to use DC Fast Charging, which gets a battery to an 80 percent charge in less than half an hour. This has the potential to reshape how Americans do long-distance drives. You could go for, say, 200 miles or so, then stop at a highway oasis with fast-charging stations and amenities. Stretch your legs, check your email, get a coffee, use the bathroom, let the dog out. Then back in the car for the next 200 miles. Rather than being a hassle, that sounds pleasant.

Is It Really Green?

As much as almost anything manufactured in this world, yes, electric vehicles are green. Car makers know that the early adopters for this technology are ecologically conscious, so they make the effort to go a bit further with things like soy-based seat foam, recycled upholstery material, and other greener choices. Plus there's that whole thing about not drilling for oil, and not shipping that oil around the world, and not burning it on the daily and sending particulates into the air. You know, that part.

There are two big hurdles to perfect greendom: the power source and the batteries. Where your power comes

What Is an Electric Vehicle?

from will make a difference in how green your EV is. If you're powering the charger with a solar array on the garage roof, you may hug as many trees as you like. Maybe someone will let you foster endangered tiger kittens for your troubles. But if your utility company draws its power from coal plants, you're not doing the planet many favors.

Speaking of raping the earth for our insatiable energy needs, those lithium ion batteries aren't made of magic and rainbows. They're made of metals—lithium is right in the name—that are mined. Once you're done with them, they need to be recycled, though there aren't that many recycling facilities right now. Tesla will take back its batteries and recycle them itself, but most communities are struggling to get anything beyond glass recycled at the curb. Shipping the batteries off to be recycled is expensive and wasteful.

The benefits of electric vehicles so outweigh the political, environmental, and public health problems of gasoline and diesel, though, that Volvo announced it would only build electrified vehicles from 2019 forward. As of 2017, the entire countries of France and the United Kingdom will no longer sell gasoline or diesel vehicles as of 2040.

What Is a Hydrogen Vehicle?

To put it really basically, a hydrogen vehicle is an electric car that can be refueled at a hydrogen fuel station rather than recharging using a plug. To be even more straightforward and practical about it, you probably can't buy a hydrogen car anyway. There are three available in 2017: Honda Clarity, Hyundai Tucson Fuel Cell, and Toyota Mirai. The first two are only available in California, which has most of the hydrogen fueling stations; the Mirai is also sold in Hawaii. All told, as of July 2017, there are thirty-seven public hydrogen stations total in the entire country.

Now for the less straightforward tech part. A hydrogen fuel cell takes liquid hydrogen fuel and oxygen from the air and makes water. The process creates electricity, which powers the batteries. The byproducts of this process are water and a bit of lost energy in the form of heat. NASA has used hydrogen fuel for decades, and astronauts drink the resulting water in space. Drinkable water is certainly an improvement over the particulates that come from the tailpipe of a car with a gasoline engine.

Hydrogen is less energy dense than gasoline, though, which means you need to store a lot of it in a big tank in order to go as far between fill-ups as you probably do in your current car. Filling up isn't exactly the same as it is with a gasoline car, either, though it is similar. Since the hydrogen fuel is a pressurized gas (not gasoline; *gas*, like not liquid or solid), there's a system of hoses and seals that need to be connected in order to fill the tank. It only takes about thirty seconds longer, but if you're freaked out by Windows updates or have a flip phone, this might not be the car for you.

Who Gets the Biggest Bang for This Buck?

Southern Californians are the only people who can really get any practical bang at all from this buck. There just isn't anywhere else in the country to refuel a hydrogen car. Even if you live in a hotbed of hydrogen fuel stations, there are only a few cars out there to have, and those are usually only leased. You can buy the Toyota Mirai, but the Honda Clarity and Hyundai Tucson are lease-only. With that lease, you usually get free hydrogen fuel, which is a plus. In the case of the Clarity, Honda works closely with customers to improve on the next generation of its fuel-cell vehicle, so if you like being part of the iteration process, that's another plus. If you want a car that's already been entirely figured out, hydrogen fuel cells are not going to be your jam.

Is It Really Green?

Hydrogen-powered cars are electric cars that use pressurized hydrogen in a tank rather than electricity from a plug, so there isn't any combustion byproduct to account for, and the process of turning hydrogen fuel into electricity only results in water.

What Is a Hydrogen Vehicle?

But that hydrogen isn't, as you might expect, pulled out of thin air. The hydrogen molecule is rarely found alone in nature, so it has to be processed. Most commonly, as it's the cheapest and easiest source to deal with, natural gas is the starting point for hydrogen fuel. Natural gas reacts with high-temperature steam or is partially oxidized to produce synthesis gas, which is further reduced to create hydrogen fuel and a little bit of carbon dioxide. The same high-temperature steam process can be used with ethanol to make hydrogen.

Water can be split into hydrogen and oxygen with an electric current, and if that current is generated via wind or solar power, then the result is about as green as fuel comes. Fermenting biomass to create hydrogen is only slightly less green on the scale. Neither of these are as cheap and easy as natural gas reforming. Way down there on the scale is gasification of coal, which also involves high-temperature steam. Then again, you can gasify biomass as well, though it's really inefficient.

Hydrogen is, for the most part, produced where it's used, so there isn't a network of pipelines and tankers delivering hydrogen fuel like there is for gasoline. Also, in order to be put into a tanker, the hydrogen gas (not gasoline, remember; *gas*) would have to be cryogenically frozen until it was cold enough to become a liquid. And then that truck has to drive on the highway next to you. Oh, the humanity.

What Is a Diesel Vehicle?

Back in the early days of the automobile, everybody and his brother (never his sister) thought they could build a better engine. The internal combustion engine we know and love and find under most hoods is called an Otto cycle engine. But not long after Nikolaus Otto built his engine, Rudolf Diesel built his.

The differences are slight—the Otto engine uses spark plugs to ignite the fuel, while the Diesel engine uses glow plugs—but they're significant enough to require slightly different forms of fuel. For decades, diesel fuel caused that smelly, black, horrid stuff that streamed out of the exhaust pipes on semitrucks. But over the years, the federal government has passed stricter regulations for emissions from diesel engines for both semitrucks and passenger vehicles. The end result is what we now call "clean diesel." It's an energy-dense fuel, so you can really rack up the miles per gallon.

Another benefit, for those with access to it, is that you can run biodiesel in most modern diesel engines. This stuff is made from old french-fry grease or other industrial veggie-oil waste. Where I live in Portland, Oregon, this caught on pretty early, and you could tell when you were following a biodiesel car not by the loud-and-proud eco-stickers all over the trunk, though those were certainly there, but by your sudden and unexplained cravings for french fries, or doughnuts, or whatever the source was for the fuel.

Who Gets the Biggest Bang for This Buck?

Diesel vehicles excel on the highway, turning in hybrid-like numbers or better in some cases. These cars work best for road warriors who travel for their jobs or take as many four-day weekends at the coast as they can squeeze out of their paid time-off days.

Diesel has gotten hard to find in the United States in the wake of the Volkswagen scandal, and it's not looking good for this fuel in the future either. A quick refresher: in the summer of 2015, researchers found that VW had used a few lines of code to cheat emissions testing. The tests are done on machines that run the engine through a pattern—fast, then slow, then accelerating hard, etc. The engineers knew the pattern, so when the car's computer recognized it, it changed the way the engine ran to reduce the emissions coming out of the tailpipe. When the test was over and normal driving resumed (turning the steering wheel was a dead giveaway to the software), the engine mapping reverted to a sportier, more fun, and dirtier profile. This was done for years in Volkswagens and Audis, and in the wake of stricter, more thorough emissions tests, several other manufacturers got caught. Not to the tune of $15 billion to right the wrongs in 500 million cars like VW, but caught cheating nonetheless. That spurred VW (and likely other manufacturers) to invest more heavily in electrified vehicles.

What Is a Diesel Vehicle?

But that's not all. In addition to France banning the sale of gasoline- and diesel-powered vehicles in 2040, four major global cities are banning diesel by 2025. Paris, Mexico City, Madrid, and Athens decided that diesel, with its particulates and nitrogen oxides, was contributing massively to the air quality issues in those cities. Not even clean diesel is clean enough.

Is It Really Green?

Diesel is still drilled out of the ground, just like gasoline. They're both products of crude oil, along with jet fuel, kerosene, and motor oil. A little more bad news: since diesel is so heavy and oily, it emits far more soot out the tailpipe, which you've surely noticed coming from older diesel engines. This leads to smog and crap in your lungs. Some manufacturers have figured out ways to counteract the soot without cheating on tests. Mercedes-Benz claims that with its BlueTEC system, you can stand directly behind the tailpipe in a white suit and not get dirty. I would probably still get dirty because I seem to be like Pigpen from *Peanuts*, but I get what they mean.

Biodiesel is gaining traction beyond the old Volvos converted by hippies to run on french fry grease. It's an EPA-approved fuel now made from recycled cooking oil, soybean oil, and animal fats. It can be used in any diesel engine without making any modifications, and it does not void any manufacturer's warranty, especially if it's a blend of biodiesel and petroleum-based diesel. The petroleum diesel—diesel classic, let's call it—helps clean out greasy deposits from the biodiesel. Diesel in any form is pretty oily, so the engines are capable of handling most of it anyway. Like ethanol blends, you'll know it by its letter and number: a 2 percent blend of biodiesel is B2; a 20 percent blend is B20.

What Is E85?

You've probably seen badges on the backs of vehicles—most often on the tailgates of full-size pickups and SUVs—saying that it's a Flex Fuel Vehicle. That means it can run on E85, a blend of gasoline and ethanol. These vehicles can also run on straight gasoline. The truth is, all of our cars are a little bit flexible this way. Some states, like Oregon where I live, blend a little ethanol, usually 10 percent, into the gasoline in winter to lower costs.

Ethanol is a plant-based fuel, and starchy plants—especially cheap and easy corn—make up nearly all of the ethanol production in the United States. The plants go through biomechanical conversion, which means the sugars are fermented into fuel.

E85 is merely the highest concentration of ethanol; it means that 51 to 85 percent of the fuel is ethanol, with the remaining percentage being gasoline. This fuel cannot be used in an engine that hasn't been modified. The manufacturer has to say it's okay. There's also E15, which is the flip of E85—it's 15 percent ethanol and 85 percent gasoline. This fuel is perfectly fine for any vehicle made after 2001 (well, not a diesel vehicle, but you knew that).

And there's E10, which you probably guessed has 10 percent ethanol blended with 90 percent gasoline. The

EPA officially calls this "substantially similar" to gasoline and can be used willy-nilly in any old gasoline-powered engine. Actually, E10 makes up more than 95 percent of all the gasoline in the country, and it's sold in every state in the union to boost octane and meet air quality requirements.

Who Gets the Biggest Bang for This Buck?

Big, fuel-hungry SUVs and pickups that cover a lot of miles are really the only vehicles that get much benefit from E85. In fact, the fuel economy drops when you put E85 in the tank of a Flex Fuel Vehicle because it is less energy dense—one gallon of E85 doesn't have the same oomph as a gallon of gasoline. Otherwise, it works exactly the same way as gasoline: same power output, same acceleration, same ability to haul around people and stuff. But using mostly corn instead of mostly fossil fuels.

Is It Really Green?

Well, um, E85 is sort of green. Mostly. But it has its issues. There's that corn thing for starters. Growing corn is a pretty harsh enterprise, and the folks growing it en masse for biofuel feedstock, as it's known, aren't growing organic heirloom varieties. They're growing industrial corn, with pesticides and the whole deal.

Which brings us to the second issue—if they're growing it for fuel, they're probably not growing it for food. Most people rely on farmers for food, not fuel. There is a concern

What Is E85?

for the global food supply if too many fields are turned over to fuel production. The industry is taking steps to move toward using waste vegetation rather than "virgin" corn, which would help the food supply situation.

There's also the fact that the tailpipe emissions aren't really any better than those from gasoline. The emissions mix may be a bit different, but the carbon dioxide that comes out of the exhaust pipe is pretty much the same. For a Suburban using gasoline, that's 521 grams of CO2 per mile; for one running on a tank of E85, that's 492 grams per mile.

What Is a Liquid Natural Gas Vehicle?

There are not many natural gas vehicles (NGVs) in America so far, but these cars are crazy popular in Iran, Argentina, Brazil, Italy, Germany—the list goes on, to the tune of more than 18 million natural gas vehicles on roads around the world. That number is expected to nearly double by 2020 to almost 35 million.

But here in the United States, sales of natural gas passenger cars were well below 3,500 in 2013, and in 2017, there are only about a thousand public refueling stations in the country. Compare that to the nearly 170,000 gasoline stations we have, and you can see how you'd have to be really committed, and geographically correct, to own a natural gas-powered car.

These cars don't use gasoline, they use—as the name implies—natural gas, the same stuff that makes the blue flames on your stovetop or powers your furnace. It's an actual gas, not a liquid like gasoline, and it's mostly methane. Because average humans need to be able to refuel their tanks without a chemistry degree and safety goggles, the gas is compressed until it becomes a liquid. Et voila! Compressed natural gas (CNG): another mysterious acronym you might have run across already.

Who Gets the Biggest Bang for This Buck?
Very few people will see any kind of savings from a CNG car, if only because very few people in the United States will see a CNG car anytime soon. If you do see one on the street, it will likely be part of a fleet of vehicles owned by the city or a utility company.

Is It Really Green?
Natural gas is green in the sense that it isn't petroleum shipped from the Middle East or extracted from Canadian tar sands, for what that's worth. Natural gas is very abundant in the United States, so it is a home-grown fuel. It also produces fewer emissions at the tailpipe, so driving is cleaner. Mercedes-Benz claims that its dual-fuel E200, which runs on either gasoline or natural gas, emits 20 percent less carbon when there's CNG in the tank than when it's running on gasoline.

But natural gas is also being fracked out of the ground at some environmental cost, which may include groundwater contamination and increased earthquake activity in formerly quiet zones. And at each step of natural gas production, refinement, and distribution, methane is leaked into the air. This is indeed the same gas that comes from cow farts, but oil and gas activities are the single largest source of methane emissions in the United States, according to the EPA.

Conclusion

Just as there isn't one fuel type that's going to solve the world's problems, there isn't one fuel type that's going to meet every driver's needs. Some want an all-electric car but they know they have to deal with hours-long traffic jams in Los Angeles. A plug-in hybrid offers a useful compromise for those drivers. Or maybe you just can't get around the fact that your job requires you to drive up and down the highway some days; a diesel engine will be easy to refuel and will get amazing mileage. And if you're a poke-around-town type, a pure EV would be a lot of fun, and it would give you plenty of opportunities for smugness.

The key is to do your research and be honest about your lifestyle. You may be dying to ditch the gas pump, but if you drive sixty miles one way over a mountain pass to get to work, an EV is not going to make you a happy person.

Like so many things we buy in the twenty-first century, cars cannot be one-size-fits-all anymore. Not only do you get to choose whether or not to add a wifi connection or nineteen-inch rims to your new ride, you get to choose the fuel that powers the whole thing—and maybe in the process make the world a better, healthier, greener place.

Part Three: Bringing Baby Home

The time has finally come to pull the trigger, write the check, and drive this thing home. Take a deep breath and bring an energy bar. This is going to be a long day.

Starting the Conversation

Here are a few low-stress factors that you can bring up to maximize your budget during the purchasing phase, even if you're not negotiating like Watto for the sale of Anakin Skywalker (Yup, I just made an obscure Star Wars reference. Nerd up!):

- **Trade in.** Bring your old car. The salesperson will evaluate it and offer you a trade-in price. This will be counted toward the price of your new car. This works best if you've paid off your old car; otherwise, make sure the trade-in price more than covers what you owe the bank.
- **Current inventory.** Dealers are more eager to sell what's on the lot than to special order a car with your exact specifications. If you test-drive a car that's close enough to what you wanted, let the salesperson know that you were hoping to get, say, a moonroof, but you'd be willing to take the car on the lot for a 15 percent discount. Let him counteroffer.
- **Good credit.** If you know you have stellar credit, like in the 700-and-up range, work it like a freakum dress. Strut your fiscal-responsibility stuff. A good credit score will get you the best interest rates, and

salespeople like to work with people who are less likely to flake on payments.

• **Down payment.** Though there are zero-down offers out there, if you've got at least 10 percent of the purchase price in cash on the day, let the salesperson know. The finance company makes money off the interest of the loan, but the salesperson will be glad to have as much cash in hand as possible.

It is important to note, until the salesperson whips out the contract and you start signing official pieces of paper, *you can walk away*. I don't mean in a mind-game way; I mean walk away. If the price isn't right, or there's a terrifying noise coming from under the hood, or the trade-in value won't cover what you've got left on the old loan, or you really need Bluetooth connectivity but the car on the lot doesn't have it, walk away. Thank the salesperson or owner for his time, smile, shake hands, and leave. Don't feel guilty for wasting his time; don't feel bad for making him spend time with you. Who wouldn't want to spend time with you and your sparkling wit? You know what you want, and that car just wasn't it. No big whoop.

As Annette Sykora told me, "It is always the woman's choice, clearly, their decision to say yes and to purchase. They shouldn't confuse a suggestion with pressure."

You can also walk away when you're being dissed by a sexist asshole. Friends of mine were in the market for an expensive new minivan this year, and when they greeted the salesman, he brushed the woman's hand out of the

Starting the Conversation

way to shake her husband's. That's when she said, "We're leaving," and her husband went with her out the door, never to return. An easy $50,000 sale to knowledgeable buyers walked out with them.

When I was shopping for a pickup a few years ago, I had heard good things about a new-car dealership downtown. I went, talked to a couple of sales guys, and took a test drive of a used truck. It was fine, but they wanted more for the truck than I could afford. I let the sales guy (I'll call him Dave Jones) know that it was more than I wanted to pay. I'd just bought a house, after all.

"Let me see what I can do," Dave said and led me inside the dealership.

I sat in a sad little waiting room with round tables and small plastic chairs. It was a Saturday afternoon, so the place was crammed with families, all waiting to see what the sales staff could do, just like me.

A few minutes later, Dave returned, mustache twitching happily, and told me that the boss had knocked a couple thousand off the price. It was still too high; really, I had no business test-driving the truck I'd driven, but I had to drive something to get the ball rolling. I told him it was still too high, and he asked what I was looking for.

"I can only afford about $250 a month," I said. I knew that for the perfect truck, I could spend a little more than that. This was my first mistake: negotiating based on the monthly payment rather than the overall price. The dealer can always stretch out terms and find ways to get you what you want—but you'll surely pay more in the long run. Do your research, create your budget, and stick to your guns.

Take The Wheel

Dave sighed; his mustache drooped. He wrote $250 on a piece of scratch paper and said, "If I can get this for you, will you buy the truck?"

"Sure." I shrugged.

"Sign here," he said and pointed at the scrap paper. I did, because I am an idiot. He disappeared into the back. I watched *Headline News* while a mom and dad tried to corral their antsy kids in Spanish next to me. I was antsy too; I felt for those kids.

Dave came back, mustache perky. "I got $300; that's the best I could do. It's a really great deal on that truck."

"It is," I agreed, "but I can't afford it. Thanks so much for your time." I rose to go.

Dave was not pleased. "But you signed this piece of paper!"

"It's just a piece of paper, and I can't afford it."

He marched to the opposite wall, where polished brass plates were mounted on a wooden plaque. He thrust a finger at one plate after another. "I'm Dave Jones. I've been the highest-selling salesperson here month after month after month. Do you see this?" He jabbed his finger again, and his face reddened.

I was not at all sure what his sales record had to do with my budget, and I was probably looking at him like he was spouting gibberish under that brushy mustache. I'm not very good at mustering a sympathetic face when I don't feel sympathetic.

"Sorry, Dave. Thank you for your time. I really appreciate it." And I left. How does a guy like that get all those brass plates? Is that his sales technique, demanding that buyers support his nameplate habit? Bizarre.

Starting the Conversation

But I learned that no one melts into a sad little puddle like the Wicked Witch of the West after turning down a salesperson's offer. You just go on to the next dealership. I also learned that Dave Jones has an unnatural attachment to brass nameplates.

If this is the car you want, and you seem to be homing in on the price you want, then of course there's no reason to walk away. Whether you're at a dealership looking at a brand-new car or in the seller's driveway about to write a check for a used car, this would be a good point to check in with your research.

Negotiation Lite

Everyone, especially women, is afraid that the rest of the world is better at negotiating than they are. Everyone else is cooler at the table, gets a better deal, isn't afraid to go for the throat.

Bull. Shit. A few people do like to negotiate, but those folks are pretty rare, and they're not all men. The truth is, most of us hate it, and it makes us nervous. Salespeople know this. But you have done your homework and checked out prices, features, and CarFax reports, so whether it's a new or used car you're going to buy today, you know what you want, what it's worth, and what you can afford. Don't let some guy in a shiny tie and pleated-front pants or some woman in a short skirt and long jacket convince you to do anything with your wallet that you didn't plan on doing before you set foot in the dealership or on the seller's lawn. Your research, your money, your car, your decision.

Buying a car is not the same as buying shoes on Zappos, where everyone is so friendly and there's free shipping both ways. A 2011 study in the United Kingdom found that women feel they're "more likely to be ripped off" by the dealership than men are. They feel patronized, and they hate even stepping foot in a dealership, so much so that

Take The Wheel

nearly half of women polled wouldn't buy a car from a dealer unless they had a man with them. That's rubbish.

Some people, especially those of the old school of car buying, will advise you to play a few mind games with the salesperson, pretending you don't want what you do want to try and get a lower price, or leaving before finalizing the sale as a scare tactic. If you're a game player naturally, go for it. Whatever injects a little fun into the tedious process of buying a car is cool. If you're not a game player, let it go. Games are not necessary, despite what we've been told.

That doesn't mean you should step from the Ford Escape you've just test-driven and declare, "The sticker price on this car is $25,000, and I have $25,000 budgeted for it. Sign me up." You could do that, but you can usually do better, even without games and swagger.

If you're at a dealership, there's a price in the window of the car; people call this the MSRP (manufacturer's suggested retail price), or the sticker price. If you're buying from a private party, there's the price listed in the classified or Craigslist ad. This number is usually your starting point for negotiations; if you're at a dealership that prides itself on skipping the negotiating process, then you can indeed skip it. Or if the seller used the word *firm* in his ad, he probably doesn't have a lot of wiggle room in the price.

But! You are an adventurous woman with a phone or folder full of information. If you want to do a wee bit of negotiating, now is the time. Start by offering 20 percent less; see if that gets you anywhere. If the car has an advertised price of $20,000, offer $4,000 less, which is $16,000. Ballsy move, right, asking someone to knock $4,000 off

Negotiation Lite

the price? Indeed, but you are nothing if not ballsy. Wait calmly. He'll tell you there's no way he can do that. He'll offer an explanation—it won't cover the dealership's costs; it won't pay off what the dude owes on the car.

That's fine; you were just feeling him out. Smile; it's your choice if that's a chipper and cheerful smile or a cat toying with a mouse kind of smile. Play to your strengths. He'll say the best he can do is $19,000. You know this probably isn't true, so you say you really like the car, and you'll just take the one right off the lot, even if it doesn't have an iPod interface, if you could get it for $17,500.

It could go on; it could stop right there. You can go back and forth with dollars and features at a dealership until you're happy and you're not stealing food from the mouths of the salesperson's children. If you're in the dude's driveway, the back-and-forth will likely be short, and either you'll agree on a price or one of you will say, "Sorry, but I just can't." If the guy (if this happens, it will be a guy) asks if you want to check with your husband/boyfriend/father before saying no to his fantastic offer, walk away faster. Flipping the bird is optional, but probably really satisfying. Welcome to the twenty-first century, bub.

That's how negotiation works. It's as simple or as arcane as you feel like making it, and as friendly or as adversarial as you can stomach. Reading *The Art of War* is entirely optional.

Wading through the Paperwork

If you're in someone's dining room exchanging paperwork and checks, finalizing the purchase is pretty easy. Make sure you get the title and that it's properly filled out, especially the odometer reading. If you're in an office in a dealership, take the salesperson up on his offer of water or coffee. If they've got popcorn, even better. This part takes *forever*.

A printer near the desk will start spitting out forms in a volume not seen in any other setting since the 1980s. Everyone else may have gone paperless, but at a car dealership, you still have to physically sign on the dotted line. A lot. They will give you a pen for this, and you can keep it if you like. Sometimes they let you keep your coffee cup too, to commemorate the hours of your life spent in the dealership that you will never get back.

The most basic thing you'll have to sign is the loan agreement. If you're buying a used car from a private seller, you probably had to go through this process at your bank or credit union. Dealerships have a finance system in place that can set up your loan through the manufacturer's financial arm or through a national bank, like Bank of America. You don't have to take the dealership's terms, by the way. If your bank or credit union will give you a killer interest rate on a car loan, take it. But often, if you want those low rates in the television commercials, you have to get the loan through the dealer.

While you're keyed up at the thought of driving home a new (or new-to-you) car and drowning in triplicate legal-size forms, the salesperson is going to start throwing extra offers at you. In my experience, none of these are freebies. If he offers a clear coat or floor mats or an air freshener, ask how much it will add to the cost of your loan.

Read, or at least carefully scan, all the contracts he shoves in front of you. Do they seem standard? Reasonable? Are the numbers what you expected to see? If any of this raises a flag, ask a question. You are not bothering the salesperson by asking, and if you are, then he's not very good at his job. You are paying the money for a car you will drive every day for several years. Make sure you understand what you are signing up for. Settle in with a second cup of coffee if you need to.

Warranties and Service Contracts

Every new car comes with a warranty of some kind, but dealerships also offer service contracts for new vehicles. There's one big difference between the two: a warranty comes with the car at no extra cost; a service contract or extended warranty is something you pay extra for.

Warranties are often trumpeted in new car ads, like Kia's and Hyundai's ten-year/100,000-mile warranties. Most cars are covered for three years or 36,000 miles, whichever comes first. That means that the cost of repairing or replacing major parts of the car, like the engine and transmission, are covered if there's some malfunction. This warranty does not cover oil changes or accidents, but it does cover repairs made because of recalls. If you get a real clunker, state lemon laws will direct you to what's written in the manufacturer's warranty to get a replacement. The manufacturer's warranty is the only one of these services that you won't pay extra for.

An extended warranty is an extension of the original manufacturer's warranty for an extra period of time or more miles. You almost always have to buy this right up front, along with the new car, though warranty companies will start sending you offers to extend the warranty when your original warranty is about to run out. It's cheaper to buy an extended warranty before yours runs out, but there's little reason to extend the warranty if your car has been reliable.

A service contract is most often between you and the dealership. This covers repair or replacement of any part that fails and usually includes extra things like tires, engine parts, and sometimes even bodywork, like banging out dents. It's quite similar to an extended warranty, so check the wording of the contract in either case to see if it's worth it to you.

A maintenance agreement only takes care of maintenance work, like oil changes and tire rotations. If something goes wrong with the vehicle, this will not help you, but if you drive more than the average American and need more frequent maintenance, this can be money well spent.

Be aware too that the contract might not be with the manufacturer or even the dealership where you're signing the paperwork and buying the car. It could be a third party that offers a lower price, but they may also be a fly-by-night outfit that will gladly take your check on vacation to Mexico. Permanently. It's been such a problem in the past that manufacturers, insurers, dealers, and legitimate contract providers have banded together to protect their sullied reputations. The Service Contract Industry Council (SCIC, to make it easier on ourselves) helps states create legislation to weed out the baddies and keep your checks from learning to surf in the Yucatán rather than paying for your contracted car repairs.

If you do decide to pay for a service contract up front, the SCIC reports that you're not alone. Over ten million

Warranties and Service Contracts

people paid for service contracts on new and used vehicles in 2012, and these contracts covered 95 percent of the claims filed that year, according to the SCIC's research.

Be careful what you pay for, as always. Sources like *Consumer Reports* will give you information on typical annual maintenance costs for a vehicle. Know that number when you walk into the dealership. The service contract will be tacked on to your car loan, so you'll be paying interest on it. If the average annual maintenance costs are close to the cost of the service contract, paying for the maintenance out of your pocket as you go will likely be less expensive.

It's Yours! Now What?

It's taken weeks of research, a couple of test drives, and an afternoon of signing papers and writing huge checks, but you finally have the car you want. Step one: crank up the radio and sing along at the top of your voice as you drive home. Make eye contact with other drivers to transmit your full happiness at crossing this huge task off your to-do list. Know you won't likely have to go through this again for at least three years if you leased, and probably something more like seven if you bought your vehicle.

When you get home, order in some Chinese because you won't feel like cooking, and while you chow down on cashew chicken, read the owner's manual. No one ever does this, but it is so worth your time. Start with the fun stuff: how to hook up your phone with Bluetooth, how to set the radio, how to turn off the traction control when you want to drift around corners like a rally driver. Then flip to the back, where there is usually a chart of important stuff: how often to change the oil and other fluids, recommended major service intervals, specs for everything from turning-signal bulbs to tires.

If you bought a brand-spanking-new car from the dealership, it probably only has delivery miles on it, maybe a couple dozen. You'll need to break in the engine, which is

Take The Wheel

a far less fraught process now than it was a few decades ago. Breaking in the engine just means that you give all those brand-new engine parts a chance to settle in properly. The rubber seals and gaskets need to warm up and fit themselves where they belong, fluids need to travel through their hoses and chambers. With the miracle of the computer age, you don't have to creep along at slow speeds for the first million miles anymore, but it is a good idea to be kind to your newborn engine, for the first few thousand miles anyway. Don't push it too hard, don't mash the pedal as soon as the light turns green, don't jack it up to 100 mph on the freeway, don't start a 3,000-mile road trip as soon as you leave the lot. Drive on highways some and on streets some. Mix it up. Your engine will thank you, and so will your wallet, when you don't have to do an engine overhaul at 30,000 miles.

If you bought an electric car, you don't even have an engine. There are no seals or valves or pistons or hoses; there are circuits and wires. You don't break in a phone or a lamp; likewise, you don't break in an EV. You can just charge it up and drive it. There are lots of settings to set and screens to check out and apps to download, but no special driving behavior is required.

If you bought a used car, it likely has at least 25,000 miles or so on it. It's been broken in—by someone else. The first week or four, it's important to notice your used car's quirks. Since you are a diligent car purchaser, you likely won't find any major issues at this point. Brakes might squeal, a cold engine might struggle, a door might creak every time you open it. Fix what you can; live with the rest.

Maintenance

After a few months of driving, you'll need to start taking care of maintenance, whether it's a new or used car. According to *Road and Travel Magazine*, 65 percent of women take their own cars in for service. But like the purchasing process itself, that doesn't mean women feel like they know what they're doing when they walk in the shop door.

Most cars built in the last decade need oil changes about every 5,000 miles (check your owner's manual to make sure) and a more comprehensive service at 30,000, 60,000, and 90,000 miles. If you bought a new car, you've got some time; if you bought a used car, be prepared to spend a couple hundred bucks on things like spark plugs and fluid changes.

Again, if you bought an EV, there's almost no maintenance. No oil. No spark plugs. No fluids. It's another benefit of all-electric driving.

Tires and brakes wear out no matter what kind of powertrain makes the car move. Brakes are often taken care of during a routine maintenance visit, but if you live in a mountainous area, you might need to get them swapped out more often. Brake pads are cheap and easy enough; you could replace them yourself with a jack and a tire iron.

Take The Wheel

Seriously. Or you can pay a little more to build rapport with your mechanic and have him change them. Regenerative braking systems in electrified cars, including hybrids and PHEVs, need professional care.

Tires are usually rated for how many miles they can travel; pay attention to how many miles you've put on them and get a new set (four at a time is best) when it's time. Don't push the tires too far; if they don't have enough tread, your stopping power will vanish, and if the steel belts inside start to show through, you're playing with your life.

There are a couple of super-easy maintenance items you can definitely take care of yourself. Windshield wipers and fluid, for example. You can get a jug of wiper fluid for a few bucks, and the reservoir is usually clearly marked inside the engine compartment. Raise the hood, fill the reservoir to the line, and feel badass about it. You can even do this in an EV. Wipers can usually be snapped or slid into place; it's so easy, you can do it in the parking lot of the auto parts store (Napa, Pep Boys, AutoZone, etc.).

If you're feeling extra badass, you can check your oil too. It's also easy. The dipstick is easy to find; it usually has a loop on the end to make it easy to remove. So when the engine is cool, remove it. Wipe it clean on a rag and put it back into the tube it came from. Take it out again, and check the bottom couple of inches of the stick. There will be oil on the dipstick and markings to tell you what's low and what's high. If you're low, you can add oil with a funnel to the reservoir (oil is another cheap and easy thing to buy), or you can ask for help from a mechanic or car-savvy friend.

Maintenance

One last easy maintenance thing to bond you with your car: coolant. This is the fluid that circulates in the engine to keep it from overheating. If you don't check the reservoir, which is as easy as checking the windshield wiper fluid, an awful lot of smoke might come from under your hood. If it's really, really empty, it can cause your engine to basically burn up and die. I should know—it's how I killed my first car when I was seventeen. You probably won't kill yours this way, since you will have purchased a far better car than a 1984 Chevy Chevette, and because when you go in for an oil change, they usually top off the coolant.

While we're discussing my Chevette, let's go over the idiot lights on the dashboard. The Chevette had two: Check Engine and Oil. The Check Engine light did indeed come on, but I ignored it in my seventeen-year-old confidence that things like that didn't apply to me. I am why they are called idiot lights.

You, being an adult non-idiot, should know a bit about the warning lights that will come on at some point. There are more things than ever before that your car can warn you about, and to varying degrees. Take, for example, the tire-pressure monitoring system that new cars have. Some systems let you know when a tire is flat or nearly flat; some let you know when a tire is low on pressure but not at a crucial stage of flatness; and others will give you a detailed in-dash diagram of which tire is low, how low it is, how much time you have to fill it up before someone looks at you funny, and how many tenths of a second it will add to your zero-to-sixty time if you don't fill it up pronto. You'll want to read up on the warning lights in the manual that came with your car.

Take The Wheel

The Check Engine light is still around, but the blessing and curse of it is in the number of things it covers. Thanks to sensors placed all around the car and powerful computers that control just about everything but the driving (and sometimes some of the driving), the Check Engine light has become the catch-all warning for anything that could go wrong with your car, from an unlatched gas cap to a thrown piston. Granted, you'll likely know that something is majorly wrong if a piston shoots out of the engine (it's rare; don't worry), but having that light come on while you're innocently driving along can cause panic. If your car is very old, has a lot of miles on it, or was in an accident, take the warning at least semi-seriously. Stop at a garage on your way home from work and have someone with a diagnostic scanner look for the code that triggered the warning. The code will tell the mechanic what's wrong, and he'll tell you how quickly it needs to be fixed. If it's the gas cap, he'll make sure it's on tight and reset the code. Easy peasy.

Twenty-first-century technology has made all of this maintenance business far, far easier. The car itself will remind you to change the oil, or top off the fluids, or put air in the tires. Some cars, like BMWs and Acuras, will call the dealership and tell them you need an oil change or even that you left your lights on and the battery is running down. (The dealership will call you and tell you to go turn off your lights.) Rather than waiting for something to go wrong and trigger the Check Engine light, the vast array of sensors in modern cars can monitor just about every system in your car and tell you when to schedule a service appointment. If your car doesn't come with these reminders, there are

Maintenance

apps out there that will help you track everything. There are also dongles that plug into the OBD-II port near the steering wheel and send data to your phone or a Google spreadsheet.

A quick tip for improving your resale or trade-in value when the time comes: keep all your service receipts. The buyer or dealership will be more likely to offer more money if they know the oil was changed according to the manufacturer's recommendations, the 60,000-mile maintenance was done, and the tires were just mounted 10,000 miles ago.

If You Make a Mistake

It happens. You buy a car, new or used, you set up the payment plan, you have it for six months, and you hate it. It's not big enough for your camping gear. Getting the kid in and out of the back seat is a nightmare. Your mom, who you take to the doctor every month, can't get in and out of the passenger seat without looking like a *Saturday Night Live* sketch about how ungraceful getting old is.

Don't forget, it's just a car. It's a pain in the ass to go through this whole buying process again, but now you're a pro, and this car is just a thing that makes your life worse instead of better. You'll have to get rid of this rotten thing, but it's true that one woman's hunk of junk is another woman's dream car. Sell the coupe to a childless woman and use the cash to buy yourself a four-door sedan.

Lemon Laws

Lemon laws are for a special case of hatred. If the new car you bought is malfunctioning, you bought a lemon. Every state has a lemon law that covers vehicles, and every state's law is different. If you are taking your car back to the dealership constantly, you're going to want to check the lemon laws for your state at LemonLawAmerica.com to see if your case is lemony enough for legal action.

Let's look at Oregon's lemon law as an example, since it seems to be similar to other laws around the country:

- The law applies to new cars still under the manufacturer's warranty.
- The problem has to be reported to the manufacturer in writing.
- The manufacturer has an opportunity to fix the problem within a year.
- If it can't be fixed, the manufacturer has to replace the car or refund its full purchase price.

Some states give the manufacturer or dealership two years to fix the problem, some apply the refund to leases and all their startup costs and fees, and some states allow

Take The Wheel

for "implied warranties," which means that you should be able to expect that something you buy brand-new should work, whether there's a written warranty or not.

Nobody's Fault but Mine

More often, if you don't like the car, it's not the manufacturer's fault. It's yours. And, twice, it's been mine. Maybe three times. Well, once it wasn't my fault—it was my parents' fault for buying me a Chevy Chevette when I didn't even want a car in the first place. *Gawd, why can't you just leave me alone, Mom? Ugh!* It was faded red, the tan plastic interior smelled funny, and I had to play with the gas pedal to convince the automatic transmission to downshift and climb up even the most mild of hills.

I had fewer excuses when I bought the Ford Escort while I was in college. I had grown up around cars and car buyers, so I thought I knew what to do. I was very wrong, in the way that twenty-year-olds often are. It was cheap and used and black, and good enough for the occasional run to the grocery store. Mostly. On good days. In the two years I suffered with that car, it stopped dead in a four-lane intersection during rush hour in a Florida downpour, it stranded my boyfriend at the time (he married me eventually) in the middle of the night in the middle of Florida's swamplands, and the fuel pump gave out.

I fixed it as best I could. I had a mechanically savvy friend help me tune up the engine in the driveway, and I took it to a mechanic for the major repairs. I sold it to a

Take The Wheel

young guy who was happy to have a cheap, used black car for a while. And so the cycle continued.

My truck, on the other hand, took a while for me to hate. I bought it to get me to work on days I didn't want to deal with the bus or the rain, and to fetch two-by-fours and haul garbage to the dump. For this, it worked well.

As usually happens, my hate began as fear. We were on a road trip through the farthest reaches of Oregon one summer, tooling along on a two-lane back road, singing along with Amy Winehouse until the CD player gave out, which it always did on hot days. Then, in the quiet of a forested road, *chunk*. As the truck changed gears to go up a hill, something in the transmission made a horrible noise that the husband and I could feel in the cabin. Fear shot up my spine, but we kept driving. Nothing was overheating, no gauges were dancing, and we were miles from town. Any town.

The town we ended up in had about three thousand people and one auto parts store, which was closed for the weekend. Unsure what to do, we decided to soldier on. Once we got home, a mechanic told me that these transmissions were prone to wearing the circular bearings into an egg shape, thus the *chunk* sound. Every time the engine got hot or there was something heavy in the back, it would make that sound.

So, to recap: the CD player was broken and the transmission was egg shaped. Then I realized the rear-wheel-drive nature of the pickup was making me slide around on wet streets. Then I feared for the life of my dog, who rode shotgun in the front seat, since that was the only seat we had besides

Nobody's Fault but Mine

the driver's seat. It was official: after two years, I hated this truck, and I was the one who had picked it out and bought it.

But my terrible experience is my—and now your—lesson to learn from. I learned to budget more realistically for my next vehicle, which allowed me to spend a bit more. I learned to really think about what I personally needed from a vehicle, not just assume I needed a truck because I had bought a house and that's what everyone does. I learned how to shop around on the internet and then shop around at area dealerships for the best price and the least condescending service. I learned to believe the idiot lights. Mostly.

Epilogue

I hope that, after using this book, you have found a car that makes you as happy as my current Subaru Impreza makes me. There are hundreds of thousands of cars sold in the United States every year, and more than half of them are now being driven by women. We should be happy about our choices and confident that we didn't screw ourselves over or get taken advantage of by some old-school idiot of a sales guy.

Even though I've spent more than a decade in automotive publishing and grew up in a car-worshipping family, I learned so much in the writing of this book. The ways women talk about cars versus the ways men do, the areas where women feel least confident, and the strategies women use while shopping for a vehicle are all as useful for me as a journalist as they are for you as a consumer. I really do talk about cars in a manly way, it turns out, so if I'm writing for women, I had better tell a story and solve a problem instead of spout numbers. Apparently, 600 hp and 600 lb-ft of torque doesn't have the same swoony effect on most of you ladies as it does on me. But if I tell you how the 2013 SRT Viper throws you backward when you hammer on the gas and how much brute force it takes to throw that short shifter from first to second at 6,000 rpm, you might take notice. Maybe.

Take The Wheel

If that still doesn't make you swoon, that's perfectly okay. There are lots of vehicles out there for people who don't care about horsepower, and they're a lot cheaper and easier to drive than a Viper. You've got the intelligence and the confidence to buy a car of your own. Now you can take the wheel.

The 5 Questions Section

5 Questions to Ask Yourself
- Do I like to drive?
- How much do I drive?
- Do I drive mostly in town or on the highway?
- Do I need a commuter car for the workweek or a getaway car for weekends?
- What's my budget, including car payment, gas, and insurance?

5 Questions to Ask the Person Giving You a Loan
- What's the best rate I can get with my credit score?
- What's the difference in rate and monthly payment for a shorter or longer loan term?
- What warranties and maintenance agreements are included?
- Are there any special rates or cash-back deals right now?
- Is there a lower rate if I set up automatic monthly payments?

5 Questions to Ask the Dealership Salesperson
- Will this vehicle fit my purposes and lifestyle?
- Are there incentives for this vehicle?

Take The Wheel

- Are the features on my must-have list available singly or only as part of a package?
- What kind of warranty is included?
- Will you perform the scheduled maintenance or service warranty claims here?

5 Questions to Ask the Private Seller

- Do you have any maintenance records for this car?
- Does it have a current title?
- Why are you selling it?
- How did you use it? Was it a commuter car or a road-trip car?
- Are there any quirks I need to know about or repairs that need to be done?

5 Questions to Ask the Mechanic

- Is there any major accident damage, especially to the frame?
- Have the fluids been changed and kept full?
- Are the tires and brakes worn?
- Does the wear on the engine seem normal for the mileage?
- What would be the first service you would recommend if I bought this car?

Acknowledgments

Lots of people helped me load the original edition of *Take the Wheel* with useful information, and lots more helped with this revision. This time around, Carly Cohen, Dehlia McCobb, and Mel Wells provided personal and professional support. It's handy to have excellent editors and proofreaders as friends.

Vinnie Kinsella at Indigo again took my words and made them pretty, thanks to his mad book design skills. Also, I always appreciate his hand-holding skills during the book production process.

And thanks to Doug, who doesn't mind when I scurry out to the studio, even on a sunny Saturday morning, to write and revise books.

Bibliography

AAA's Daily Fuel Gauge Report. Accessed 2014. http://fuelgaugereport.aaa.com/.

Alternative Fuels Data Center. "Ethanol Feedstocks." US Department of Energy. Accessed 2013. http://www.afdc.energy.gov/fuels/ethanol_feedstocks.html.

———. "Biodiesel Production and Distribution." US Department of Energy. http://www.afdc.energy.gov/fuels/biodiesel_production.html.

———. "Hydrogen Production and Distribution." US Department of Energy. http://www.afdc.energy.gov/fuels/hydrogen_production.html.

Appel, Tom. "How Plug-in Hybrid Cars Work." HowStuffWorks.com, January 29, 2007. http://auto.howstuffworks.com/car-models/plug-in-hybrids/plug-in-hybrid-car.htm.

Auto Editors of Consumer Guide. "1955–1956 Dodge La Femme." HowStuffWorks.com, October 15, 2007. http://auto.howstuffworks.com/1955-1956-dodge-la-femme.htm.

Auto Remarketing Staff. "AutoTrader.com: Women Influence More than 80% of Vehicle-Purchasing Decisions." Auto Remarketing, October 4, 2010. http://www.autoremarketing.com/content/trends/autotradercom-women-influence-more-80-vehicle-purchasing-decisions.

Bilek, Mark. "5 Extended Warranty Tips." HowStuffWorks.com, October 21, 2005. http://auto.howstuffworks.com/buying-selling/cg-extended-warranty-tips.htm.

Take The Wheel

"Biodiesel Basics." Biodiesel.org. Accessed September 18, 2017. http://www.biodiesel.org/what-is-biodiesel/biodiesel-basics.

Bland, Marc. "Women Driving Increased Auto Sales." *Polk* (blog), March 23, 2011. http://blog.polk.com/blog/blog-posts-by-marc-bland/women-driving-increased-auto-sales.

Chapman, Mary M. "Online Upstarts Seek to Disrupt Used-Car Buying." *New York Times*, April 13, 2017. https://www.nytimes.com/2017/04/13/automobiles/wheels/online-used-car-sales.html.

Chrisafis, Angelique, and Adam Vaughan. "France to Ban Sales of Petrol and Diesel Cars by 2040." *Guardian*, July 6, 2017. https://www.theguardian.com/business/2017/jul/06/france-ban-petrol-diesel-cars-2040-emmanuel-macron-volvo.

Clark, Josh. "Is Hydrogen Fuel Dangerous?" HowStuffWorks.com, May 19, 2008. http://auto.howstuffworks.com/fuel-efficiency/alternative-fuels/dangerous-hydrogen-fuel.htm.

Dumitrache, Alina. "Women Hate the Car-Buying Process, Study Says." *autoevolution*, August 16, 2011. http://www.autoevolution.com/news/women-hate-the-buying-car-process-study-says-37977.html.

Frank, Michael. "Summer-Blend vs. Winter-Blend Gasoline: What's the Difference?" *Popular Mechanics*, October 15, 2012. http://www.popularmechanics.com/cars/a3180/summer-blend-vs-winter-blend-gasoline-whats-the-difference-13747431/.

Fogoros, Tina. "'Heels and Wheels' Puts Women in the Driver's Seat." IHS Markit, January 26, 2012. http://blog.ihs.com/heels-and-wheels-puts-women-in-the-drivers-seat.

Gardner, Greg. "New-Car Loans Keep Getting Longer." *USA Today*, June 1, 2015. https://www.usatoday.com/story/money/cars/2015/06/01/new-car-loans-term-length/28303991/.

Garthwaite, Josie. "For Natural Gas-Fueled Cars, Long Road Looms Ahead." *National Geographic*, September 4, 2013. http://news.nationalgeographic.com/news/energy/2013/09/130904-long-road-ahead-for-natural-gas-cars/.

Bibliography

Healey, James R. "Average New Car Price Zips 2.6% to $33,560." USA Today, May 4, 2015. https://www.usatoday.com/story/money/cars/2015/05/04/new-car-transaction-price-3-kbb-kelley-blue-book/26690191/.

"How Expensive Is Hydrogen Fuel for Cars: Price and Costs Involved." CarsDirect.com, October 31, 2012. http://www.carsdirect.com/green-cars/how-expensive-is-hydrogen-fuel-for-cars-price-and-costs-involved.

"Hydrogen Energy." RenewableEnergyWorld.com. Accessed September 18, 2017. http://www.renewableenergyworld.com/rea/tech/hydrogen.

Johnson, L. James. "Do Women Feel Disadvantaged When Buying Cars?" The Car Connection. Last modified January 31, 2011. http://www.thecarconnection.com/news/1054613_do-women-feel-disadvantaged-when-buying-cars.

LeaseTrader.com. "Women Are More Thorough Than Men When Shopping for a Car." Press release. January 19, 2012.

LeBeau, Phil. "Americans Holding onto Their Cars Longer Than Ever." CNBC.com, July 29, 2015. http://www.cnbc.com/2015/07/28/americans-holding-onto-their-cars-longer-than-ever.html.

Lemon Law America. Accessed September 18, 2017. http://www.lemonlawamerica.com/.

McGrath, Matt. "Four Major Cities Move to Ban Diesel Vehicles by 2025." BBC News, December 2, 2016. http://www.bbc.com/news/science-environment-38170794.

Nice, Karim, and Jonathan Strickland. "How Fuel Cells Work." HowStuffWorks.com, September 18, 2000. http://auto.howstuffworks.com/fuel-efficiency/alternative-fuels/fuel-cell.htm.

Office of Transportation and Air Quality. "Greenhouse Gas Emissions from a Typical Passenger Vehicle." Ann Arbor, MI: US Environmental Protection Agency, 2011 and 2014.

Take The Wheel

Rivero, Justine. "The Top 6 Misconceptions About Credit Scores." *Forbes*, March 29, 2012. http://www.forbes.com/sites/moneywisewomen/2012/03/29/the-top-6-misconceptions-about-credit-scores-2/.

Seaman, Kirk. "Check the Manual (Transmission): Stick Shift Cars Going Away." Autoblog.com, February 26, 2010. https://www.autoblog.com/2010/02/26/stick-shift-love-affair/.

Siegel Bernard, Tara. "Car Dealers Wince at a Site to End Sales Haggling." *New York Times*, February 10, 2012. http://www.nytimes.com/2012/02/11/your-money/car-dealers-wince-at-a-site-to-end-sales-haggling.html.

Siler, Steve. "Pump It Up: We Refuel a Hydrogen Fuel-Cell Vehicle." *Car and Driver*, November, 2008. http://www.caranddriver.com/features/pump-it-up-we-refuel-a-hydrogen-fuel-cell-vehicle.

Stenquist, Paul. "Natural Gas Waits for Its Moment." *New York Times*, October 29, 2013. http://www.nytimes.com/2013/10/30/automobiles/natural-gas-waits-for-its-moment.html.

"Three Manufacturers Have Record Transaction Prices; Industry Incentives Climb Slightly in May According to TrueCar.com." TrueCar.com, June 1, 2012. http://www.truecar.com/blog/2012/06/01/three-manufacturers-have-record-transaction-prices-industry-incentives-climb-slightly-in-may-according-to-truecar-com/.

Voelcker, John. "Can Hydrogen Fuel-Cell Vehicles Compete with Electric Cars?" *Popular Science*, December 6, 2013. http://www.popsci.com/article/cars/can-hydrogen-fuel-cell-vehicles-compete-electric-cars.

Wiesenfelder, Joe. "E85: Will It Save You Money?" *Long Island Press*, August 5, 2010. http://archive.longislandpress.com/2010/08/05/e85-will-it-save-you-money/.

"Women and the Automotive World." *Road and Travel Magazine*. Accessed September 18, 2017. http://www.roadandtravel.com/newsworthy/newsandviews04/womenautostats.htm.

Bibliography

WomenCertified.com. "Women's Choice Award." February 2012. https://www.womenschoiceaward.com/awarded/automotive/dealerships/darcars-frederick/.

Yvkoff, Liane. "Technology Lures Women Car Buyers." CNET, June 6, 2011. http://reviews.cnet.com/8301-13746_7-20068749-48.html.